Lost and Found

Prose and Poetry

S‍HIRLEY W‍ILLIAMS H‍OMES

Copyright © 2005 by Shirley Williams Homes.

By this author: On Dry Land, a novel
Cover design: Robin Sherwood Armour
Author image: Herbert Homes
Library of Congress Number: 2005900891

ISBN: Hardcover   1-4134-7206-0
            Softcover   1-4134-7205-2

All rights reserved. No part of this book may be reproduced or transmitted in any form or by any means, electronic or mechanical, including photocopying, recording, or by any information storage and retrieval system, without permission in writing from the copyright owner.

This book was printed in the United States of America.

Memoirs of a Reluctant Psychic first appeared in Global City Review #12

Head of the Table first appeared in Girls: An Anthology published by Global City Press

GC: Wise Women

    To order additional copies of this book, contact:
        Xlibris Corporation
        1-888-795-4274
        www.Xlibris.com
        Orders@Xlibris.com

24578

Dedication

For Herb, my husband, my friend and the love of my life
with gratitude for his integrity, his humor
and his unfailing generosity of spirit

Contents

June	Story	11
The Train to Paris	Poem	34
The Poem About the Train to Paris	Poem	35
Burgess Shale	Poem	36
Cardiff Walls	Poem	37
Andrea Doria	Poem	38
The Lesson	Poem	39
Head of the Table	Memoir	40
Brother	Poem	46
Cows	Poem	47
Bathroom Mirror	Poem	49
Mother at Eighty Three	Poem	50
DNA	Poem	51
Ceremony	Poem	52
August 1943	Poem	53
String of Pearls	Poem	54
Mine	Story	55
The Arch	Poem	67
Spy	Poem	68
Say So	Poem	69
Parentheses	Poem	70
Not Sacrifice	Poem	71
The Car	Story	72
The Well	Story	85
Island Water	Poem	104
Daytrippers	Poem	105

Black-crowned Night Heron	Poem	106
Auger Moon	Poem	107
Vacation	Poem	108
Weekend on Nantucket	Poem	109
Sea Change	Poem	110
Madaket Road	Poem	111
July After Millie	Poem	112
Summer House in Winter	Poem	113
Memoir		114
Incident in Woods	Poem	157
Old Women	Poem	158
November Heat Wave	Poem	160
Shopping List	Poem	161
The Usual	Poem	162
Safe	Poem	163
Orrie	Story	164
Basket for Edith	Poem	174
At the 'Y' with Edith	Poem	175
From the Window of the Metroliner New York to Washington, D. C.	Poem	176
The Ice House	Memoir	178
Central Park Zoo	Poem	193
82nd Street Off Lex in June	Poem	194
Encounter in February Outside the Church	Poem	195
City Fix	Poem	196
Water Stone	Poem	197
The Slots	Story	198
Parrot	Poem	218
Hocus Pocus	Poem	219
For Grace at Her Easel	Poem	220
Memoir of a Reluctant Psychic		221
Half Moon Soup	Poem	243
The Tuscan Sun	Poem	246

Basil's World .... Poem 248
Harold Godfrey Montgumery .... Memoir 250
My Mother's Body .... Memoir 252
The Cowboy .... Memoir 256

Acknowledgements 261

JUNE

A Story

"Damn! They're dead. All the fireflies are dead."

I was dreaming about school. The teacher was holding up a paper and saying it was the best in the class. I was hoping it was mine, but my brother's voice yelling about fireflies woke me up so now I'll never know. Wolf is a year younger than I am. He's nine. He's named for Grandma Wolfson, my mother's mother. He gets teased a lot. We're at the lake for the summer. Lake Pocatapaug. It's an Indian word. I don't know what it means. My father put up a tent for him and my mother to sleep in. Wolf and I sleep in a trailer my father and my grandfather built in grampa's barn. It has bunk beds. I sleep on the bottom. There's a sink and a couch and a table that folds down. There's just a big metal box for keeping food cold. We put a chunk of ice in it every couple of days. But there's no bathroom. We have to go over to the Boy Scout camp ground to use the privy. All the spiders and the stink. I hate camping. My mother knows I do but she says I should be a good sport. I hate being a good sport more than anything. It just means you have to do something you really don't want to do and you can't complain about it. Everybody else loves to spend the summer in this big field by the lake that my father rents year round from the man that owns the gas station. He owns a lot of land and he rents acre lots to families in the summer and to hunters in the winter. "Great deer country," my father always says. Maybe so, but I don't want to look at any more dead deer. We've been eating venison all winter and I'm sick of it. It tastes like blood no matter how long my father lets it hang. "These are hard times," my mother says when I tell her I won't eat any more venison stew. "We're lucky to have such good food. There are little girls and boys all over this country who don't have enough to eat." I know all about it. It's a depression and there are hungry people everywhere. They can have my venison.

"Well, what did you expect? Of course they're dead. You only punched about three holes in that lid. They suffocated. You are so dumb it hurts me to look at you," I say, sitting up and grabbing the Hellman's Mayonnaise jar from my brother's hand. He looks sad. "He loves every living thing," Grandma Wolfson says when he brings a snake or a toad into her house. I don't think she really likes the slimy things but she never makes him get rid of them.

"It's okay, Wolf. We'll get some more tonight and we'll punch enough holes and put some grass in the bottom of the jar. Is Mom up yet?" I say to change the subject and because I'm hungry.

I'm always hungry. Sometimes my stomach is so empty it wakes me up and I have to go get a bowl of Shredded Wheat in the middle of the night. My mother says I'm growing like a weed and there isn't enough food in the world to fill me up. I think she might be right. I have my own flashlight that I keep under my pillow. My mother puts a big old cooking pot on the ground outside the door of the trailer so I don't have to go all the way over to the privy to go to the bathroom in the night. My mother used to make beef barley soup in that pot but she doesn't use it for cooking any more.

I wait until Wolf has gone out of the trailer to get dressed. I don't like getting dressed with anybody around. My clothes are mostly in a box under my bunk. Shorts and shirts and underwear. We never get dressed up out here. Sometimes we wear the same clothes for three days. I change my underpants, though. And my socks. I like to feel clean. The man who owns the land we're on has a washing machine on the porch of his house. My mother takes our clothes over there once a week and washes them. Then she hangs them to dry on a line my father strung between two trees. When I pull my shirt over my head I can smell the fresh air and the sun.

"Good morning, honey. It's another beautiful day. Maybe you and I could go for a swim later," my mother says as she measures water into the coffee pot. She'll put the pot on a kind of metal stand my father made for cooking. The stand goes right over the coals of the fire he makes every morning in the fire pit beside their tent. My mother looks pretty. She always looks pretty, but especially when she lets her hair down the way she does out here at the lake. Her hair is brownish red, auburn my father calls it, and it's down to her waist when she combs it out. She wears halter tops and shorts and she goes barefoot most of the time. We do too, Wolf and I. "Like little heathen," Grandma Wolfson says. She makes it sound like a wonderful thing to be.

My mother goes into the trailer to get bread for toast. My father has walked over to the general store to get milk. He took Wolf with him. The store is about ten minutes away, down the dirt track and out across the paved road. We can't go there by ourselves because a lot of trucks use the paved road and my mother says they go 'like a bat out of you know where'. She doesn't curse but my father does. So does Wolf.

"I'm going down to the lake, Mom. I'll be back in a minute," I call.

My mother doesn't answer so I walk away down the path that ends at the dock. We swim from the dock and my father keeps our canoe tied up there. Wolf and I pretend we're

Indians when we're out on the lake paddling along. It's about the only time I can stand to play with him. Mostly he just wants to run and knock into things and yell. I'm too old for all his nonsense. All I really want to do is read but my parents think it's a waste of time or something. "Go out in the fresh air, honey. You're so pale. You need some sun and exercise. At least take your book out to the hammock." Sure, to the hammock. Where Wolf can dump me on the ground every five minutes and the mosquitoes can eat me alive. I want to stay in the trailer, on my bunk, with a glass of lemonade, my book and no bugs. That doesn't happen very often.

The water is so still this morning I could walk right out on it, like ice or glass. When I'm alone and quiet like this I almost like camping. Oh, my gosh, that's a snake. A water moccasin, I'll bet. I'm never swimming in this lake again.

"Mom, a snake. Right near the dock. Daddy better kill it," I yell as I run back up to the campsite.

"Those little water snakes are harmless, honey. Here, have some toast and an orange. The men will be right back with the milk, but I know how hungry you get. Go ahead and start."

She always calls my father and Wolf 'the men'. I wonder why she never calls us 'the women'. I'm reading "Little Women" right now. It's good, but it's sad. I wish I were like Jo. She's not afraid of anything.

My father and Wolf took the canoe out after breakfast. They asked me to come, but they didn't insist so I said I thought Mom and I were going for a swim. I've been lying here in the hammock ever since, not even reading. Just looking up at the trees and the little bit of sky I can see from here. There's a breeze so the bugs aren't too bad. I can hear birds talking to themselves and shifting around in the branches. They don't fly around much in the afternoon. I can hear my mother, too. She's in the tent fussing around with I don't know what and humming to herself. She peeked out at me a while ago but she didn't say anything. This is just so nice I wish it would never end. Except I'm hungry.

I get out of the hammock and walk toward the trailer to see if there's a Hostess cupcake left. I love the chocolate ones with the squiggly line of white down the middle of that thick chocolate frosting. You can lift the frosting right off whole and save it for after you eat the cupcake. I can just taste the way the chocolate cake wads up in my mouth, thick and sweet before I swallow. I'm right at the door to the trailer ready to step up on the wooden crate we use for a step when I hear my mother's voice.

"Company, honey. Come see," she calls. "It's a surprise."

If it was family she wouldn't be calling me. They'd be coming over to the trailer. I really don't like company. Especially people I don't know. Relatives are okay. I like it when my cousins come or my grandma.

"Honey, come on over here and meet June. She and her parents just got here," my mother calls.

I look over to where my mother is standing just outside the tent flap. I see a big man in a flannel shirt and shorts. His face looks like raw meat, red and sweaty, and his hands look like giant's hands hanging loose at his sides. He looks mean and I don't want to get close to him. I walk as slowly as I can without being rude. I can't see anybody who might be this June my mother wants me to meet.

"Well, hello there, young lady. I know your daddy from work. He's the one put us on to these camp sites. He sure brags on you. Smart little thing, according to him. Nose in a book and all. This here is June. She turned ten at Christmas. Maybe you can get her to open a book," the huge man says, talking in the direction of my mother. Not really looking at me. My mother looks pink in the face from the heat or maybe she's as shy of this man as I am.

He steps to the side, closer to my mother. She backs off into the tent opening and then I see the girl who's been standing behind her father. I see June.

She's big. That's the first thing I think. She's my age and she's almost as tall as my mother. She's big around, too, so you'd think she was a grown up except her face is pudgy and round like a baby's face and that's what she really looks like. A fat baby, kind of pretty with her pink cheeks and her big eyes. There's purple around her mouth like she just finished a grape popsicle. She's just standing there staring at me and I'm staring back. One of us is going to have to talk, but I'm not ready to yet.

Her hair is dark, almost black, and it's hanging around her face. She needs a couple of barrettes and a good scrub in the lake with Ivory soap like we do when we go swimming. Her shorts are bright red and they don't really fit. They're so tight at the cuff that her skin bulges out. It looks like it hurts. That makes me want to talk. I hate to see anybody hurt. It upsets my stomach.

"Hi," I say. "Want to go down to the lake?"

"Sure," she says, kind of rough like she doesn't care.

"We can sit on the dock. Want a cupcake?" I say, so hungry my legs are wobbly.

"What kind?" she says. Not yes, but what kind, like if I don't say the right thing she won't have one. I'm never that fussy.

"Hostess," I say. I wish they were just some plain kind of cupcake, vanilla or orange. Anything but chocolate. She doesn't deserve chocolate I decide for no real reason. Just a feeling. My mother says that sometimes when she can't explain something. Or doesn't want to. "Just a feeling I have."

"Good," she says and I head for the trailer.

She follows right on my heels. I hate when people get that close. I don't even know her, for Pete's sake, and she's walking right into the trailer like she's been asked.

"Who sleeps in here? This is a hinky setup. Doesn't look like anything I ever saw before. We sleep in a big tent with real beds and a stove and a rug on the floor and everything. This looks hinky," she says walking through the trailer, touching everything, poking behind things.

Sounds to me like 'hinky' is her word of the week. That's what my mother says when I try out new words. "That your word of the week, honey?" I like the sound of words and I try out new ones all the time. I never heard of 'hinky', though. I bet she made it up. I can't wait to get out of here. I see there aren't any cupcakes so I grab a couple of apples and get out the door as fast as I can. I don't even try to answer her.

I'm halfway down to the dock when she comes to the door of the trailer and yells, "Wait up, can't you? What's your hurry?"

I'm sitting at the end of the dock with my feet hanging over about a foot above the water, when she plops down beside me. The dock shakes like a boat hit it.

"This is really uncomfortable," she says, hitching her bottom up to the edge of the dock and letting her feet dangle beside mine.

"You'll get slivers," I say. "You have to just sit and stay put. The wood is splintered."

I'm being as nice as I can and all she's done so far is complain. This is going to be the worst summer of my life.

June looked kind of disgusted when I handed her an apple but she didn't say anything about it not being a cupcake. She ate it in a couple of bites and didn't even clean off the core, just threw it in the lake. What a waste. I was finished way before she was but my core was clean and I threw it back into the bushes beside the lake for the birds to eat. We didn't talk at all. She just said "See ya" when she pushed herself up and walked off back to her own campsite. Maybe she won't want to come back. Okay with me.

We're in the canoe, my mother in the bow, Wolf and me in the middle and my father in the stern. After supper Wolf said he wanted to go to the Arcade at the end of the lake and my mother said we could. It will be light for three more hours and it's not too long a trip by canoe. By car around the edge of the lake it's a long ride. The Penny Arcade is a wonderful place with pinball machines and a cotton candy stand and a machine that you put your penny in and then you turn a wheel and a toy steam shovel moves around over all the prizes in the glass case. You let the shovel drop when you've got it over the prize you want and maybe the teeth of it will grab your prize and drop it down a chute to you. There are watches and rings and candy bars and celluloid dolls and other things hidden at the bottom of the pile that you can only guess. I've never gotten anything but a piece of penny candy. There's a Scout knife that Wolf really wants. I know that's why he asked if we could go over to the Arcade. My father gives us ten cents in pennies when we get there and we can do whatever we want with it. It's the most money we ever get at one time except for birthdays when Grandma Wolfson gives us a dollar in our birthday card. Wolf will spend all his pennies on the steam shovel and I know he'll never get that old knife. My father says everything but the penny candy is glued down, but Wolf doesn't want to hear him. I might look around and see what else is there. Maybe a candy apple. I love the way the candy skin crackles and breaks when you take the first bite and the way the sweet makes the apple taste sour.

    Wolf is sitting behind me in the canoe. He wiggles a lot and makes the canoe dip to the side. With all four of us in it the canoe rides very low in the water anyway and his jiggling around makes me think water will come into the boat. It doesn't, and I lean back against the cane seat and look up at the sky. It's clear blue. No clouds. Light at the top and darker toward the trees along the shore. Even though it's still early some of the houses along the shore have their dock lights on. It's like magic, us in our canoe moving so quickly and quietly, and the people in the houses doing whatever they're doing, not knowing we're out here on the water looking at their lights. That's what Grandma Wolfson says God does, watches us when we don't know it. That's too scary to think

about, somebody knowing everything you do. I'd rather think it's magic.
 I'm watching my mother paddle. She was wearing one of my father's old shirts but she took it off and now she's just in her halter and shorts with her hair tied back with one of my ribbons. I can see the muscles in her back. They come up under her skin like ropes when she dips her paddle and then they disappear when she rests. Her skin is brown, even and smooth like she was born that color. My father and Wolf and I burn and peel and burn and peel all summer, but Mommy is brown in April. All she has to do is work in our garden for an hour and she's tan. Even in the middle of the winter you can see where her silver bracelet goes, on her wrist. She doesn't wear her watch in the summer. "What's time to a turtle?" she always says. I laugh every time she says it. She has a very smooth stroke with her paddle. My father likes that a lot. He always tells her what a good first mate she is. The water drips off the end of her paddle when she lifts it up out of the lake for her next stroke. The drops hitting the surface of the lake and then the paddle pushing the dark water back in ripples is the best sound in the world. I think about it sometimes in the winter just before I fall asleep.
 "Wake up, sleepy head. We're here," my father says.
 We're tied up at one of the three public docks at the Arcade. I slept almost all the way. Wolf is on the dock jumping up and down.
 "Come on. Let's go. What are we waiting for?" he's yelling.
 My mother puts her hand on his shoulder and shushes him. He won't be shushed.
 "Get out of there, you. Let's go to the steam shovel." He pushes his face at me from where he stands and I think maybe he'll lose his balance and fall in the lake. He can swim so he won't drown but he might shut up.
 There are Christmas tree lights strung from all the trees around the big old shed and the sign hanging over the open

front is painted on a wooden board with each letter outlined with lights. "PENNY ARCADE" it says.

My father and Wolf walk off to the steam shovel and my mother and I begin to wander through the aisles. It's Tuesday so there aren't too many people. Week-ends are really crowded when all the fathers come for their two days off and bring their kids here for a treat. This is one of my father's weeks of vacation. He gets another week in August. Because he's so well thought of, my mother says. Grandma Wolfson says it's because the shop is so slow in August but I think my mother's right. I usually agree with my grandmother but she guesses wrong about my father sometimes.

"Come see, honey. Look at this," my mother calls.

She's walked ahead of me and now she's stopped in front of a big table draped with red, white and blue cloth. I hurry over to her and look down to see what she's pointing at. There are thirty, forty, maybe fifty, china vases and little china people and china dogs all spread out on the cloth. They are the most beautiful things I've ever seen. So small and so perfect. My mother is holding a deep purple vase, the color of a plum. It's about three inches tall and perfectly shaped to hold tiny flowers. She hands it to me.

"Feel that, darling. Feel the raised flowers? Such workmanship. Just look," she says leaning over me and touching the red and yellow flowers on the sides of the vase.

"There's gold, too, Mommy. These little squiggles are real gold. Look how shiny they are."

I hold the beautiful vase in the cup of my hand and I'm not the least bit afraid I'll drop it. It belongs right where it is. In my hand.

"These things are all from China," the woman standing behind the table says. "Straight from China where they know how to make porcelain. I can let you have that vase for fifteen cents."

Fifteen cents! I'm ready to say I'll take it and then I

remember that all I have is ten cents for the whole night. I put the vase back on the table, standing it straight up next to a beautiful china Chinese lady. China, Chinese, I think. Nice the way the words go in and out of each other. I turn away from the table but my hand feels empty where the vase was supposed to be.

"Sometimes we just enjoy the beauty of a thing, sweetheart. We can't always own it. I'm sorry," my mother says. "Daddy gave you all the money we could spare for tonight. Maybe you'll find something else you want. Come on. We've only started to look."

She takes my hand and we stroll through the rest of the aisles. I want a candy apple but I decide to save my pennies for the next time. Maybe the vase will still be there.

"Look who we ran into," my father says when we meet him at the steam shovel. "Should have thought to ask you fellows along," he says to the people standing with him.

It's June and her father and a tiny little woman just an inch or so bigger than me who must be June's mother. We'd have sunk the canoe if we tried to bring them all with us. Now June's going to spoil one of my really favorite summer things. She's going to horn in on the Penny Arcade.

"You two girls go along and have fun. We'll find you when it's time to go," my father says.

I can't believe how angry I feel. How could he not know that I don't want a strange girl tagging along tonight. Especially a strange girl who does nothing but complain.

June starts off down the aisle and I follow, my mother's hand pushing on my shoulder. She probably thinks it's just a little push but it feels like a real shove to me.

"Got any money?" June says over her shoulder.

I decide to say I haven't so I can save it. It's none of her business anyway.

"No spending money," I say, making it just a white lie.

"I've got plenty for both of us. My father gives me money all the time."

She pulls a red change purse out of her shirt pocket and opens it. There are dollars in it. Crumpled up dollars. She snaps the purse shut again and stuffs it into the back pocket of her shorts.

"I think it's five dollars. Five or six. There's some change in there too," she says.

She's heading off down the aisle where the Chinese table is. I don't want her to see my vase. With all that money she'll buy it for sure.

"Let's go to the food counter in the back. If we go this way we can look at the stuffed animals," I say, walking over to the side of the Arcade, to the aisle that leads back to the cotton candy machine. I don't even look to see if she is following.

"Okay," she says, "I'm not very hungry but I'll get you something if you want."

That's the first really nice thing she ever said to me. She's trailing after me, stopping to look at every booth and table on the way. Good thing I got her to come this way. She'd want my vase for sure.

We stop at the booth where you throw a baseball at some wooden milk bottles and if you knock them over you get a stuffed dog. My father tried to get one for me last summer but no luck. He says they nail the bottles down.

"Bet I can do it," June says. She digs her change purse out and snaps it open. She finds a nickel at the bottom and plops it on the counter. "Gimme three balls," she says like she's done this before. "Rude," Grandma Wolfson would say if she could hear her tone of voice. Tone of voice is very important to Grandma Wolfson.

"Okay, little lady, let's see you knock those bottles for a loop," the woman behind the counter says. She's thin and wrinkled and looks like a witch until she picks up the nickel and puts it in the pocket of her apron. Then she smiles and shows her tiny white teeth, perfect, in a perfect row. She looks happy now and not like a witch at all. Like she was a friend of my mother's or my grandmother's.

June takes one of the beat up old baseballs the woman puts on the counter and steps back. She winds up just like Wolf does when he pitches to Daddy. I never saw a girl do that before. When she lets go of the ball her arm is way up in the air. Overhand. She throws overhand and she hits the pyramid of milk bottles right square in the middle. They don't fall though. Well, one does. The top one. But the rest of them are still there, solid as a rock, not even teetering.

"Great arm, young lady. You can really peg that ball. You won anything you want from the bottom row," the woman says and then she starts to yell to the people going by. "Winner here. We got a winner here. Just a kid and she's a winner. Try your luck, ladies and gentlemen, try your luck."

Just a kid but she's looking the woman right in the eye. I think June's a whole head taller than I am. She's standing there now, bent forward, studying the stuff on the bottom row. Junk, it looks like to me. Still, there is a cute little pink bear way over in the back. I wonder if she sees it.

"I'll take the cigarette case. The silver one on the second shelf. My Daddy smokes and he'd like that," she says.

"Bottom shelf, honey. One bottle is bottom shelf," the woman says, looking like a witch again.

June opens her change purse and takes out a wrinkled dollar. She puts it on the counter and says, "I want the cigarette case."

"It's yours, sweetie pie. One cigarette case coming up."

The woman picks up the cigarette case and slams it on the counter in front of June. "You're too smart by half, Tubby. Get along and bother somebody else."

"You want to try?" June says to me, ignoring the woman, not moving from where she's standing in front of the booth.

"No thanks," I say and walk away down the aisle.

I guess June doesn't care what anybody says. She stood right up to that lady. She didn't even seem to hear what she called her. I was too scared to move and she wasn't even talking to me.

"Come on, I'll get you a cotton candy," June says and leads the way to the back of the Arcade like she's been coming here all her life. Far as I know this is her first time. We stand in front of the cotton candy machine watching the man in the white coat twirl a paper cone close to the spinning threads of pink sugar. The threads catch onto the cone and in a second there's the fluffy ball of cotton candy, perfect. The man twists it once more to break it away from the web of sugar. He hands it to June who hands him a nickel.

"Want this? I'll get another one for me," she says.

I don't know what to say. I want it. I can taste the sweet spun sugar, grainy on my tongue, but I'm not comfortable to be taking anything from June. The ten pennies in my pocket feel like they weigh a ton and I'm sure if I move to take the cotton candy June will hear them clanking together. I wish I hadn't lied about having any money.

"Take it," she says, pushing the paper cone at me.

I take it and I say "Thank you" but the words are hard to say. I wish I was with Wolf and my mother and father. I can't even see where they are in the crowd. More and more people are coming and I can see that it's getting dark outside the Arcade. We'll have to go home soon.

"I think we better look for our parents. It's getting late," I say.

"They don't care how long I stay. We'll be here till midnight probably," she says. "We drove over in our new Pontiac. We get a new car every year."

We've been walking along the back of the Arcade as we talk, eating our cotton candy. June eats hers in about three bites and throws the paper cone on the floor of the arcade. I'm eating mine really slow, pulling a bit off with my lips and letting it dissolve on my tongue. June acts like she doesn't even like what she eats. A new car every year, for gosh sakes. We've never had a brand new car. She probably eats stuff like shrimps and mushrooms and chocolate eclairs all the time.

There are food booths and booths with magazines and

cigars and cigarettes back here. It's boring if you're not going to buy anything. June stops at a tobacco booth and says, "Give me a pack of Camels, please. They're for my father. He's over there," she says waving her hand off toward the front of the building.

She puts her crumpled money on the counter and the old man behind the counter picks it up, counts it, gives her her change before he slips the pack of Camels into a brown paper bag with a packet of matches that says 'Draw Me' on the cover. There's a picture of a black haired woman. She's the one you're supposed to draw. I don't know if you win a prize or what and I wonder if June's father will draw her.

"Don't tell anybody about the cigarettes," June says to me. "After all I bought you a cotton candy so you can't tell."

She has put the cigarette case she won into the brown bag with the Camels.

"Give me two Hershey bars, too," she says and puts the change the man gave her into his hand. He gives her the candy and she puts it into the paper bag, leaving the top open so all you can see is the Hershey bars sticking up. "Just keep your mouth shut," she says and walks off down the outside aisle pushing her way past the other people trying to get a look at the stuff in the booths.

I walk down the middle aisle. I want to look at my vase once more before we go home but I won't stop. I'll just walk on by in case June's watching me. There it is right next to the Chinese man and woman. They're made of the same china as my vase and they have on robes with wide belts and their eyes are slanted. They are very beautiful. Strange looking but beautiful. But not as gorgeous as my vase. Please, please, please stay there until I can save a nickel. June probably would have given me five cents, but I don't want to take anything more from her. Cigarettes! Boy, she's brave. I think she's going to smoke them herself. I wonder what that's like, what it tastes like. My mother doesn't smoke but my father has a pipe and I love the smell of it. Sweet and thick and it clings to your throat when you breath it in. Maybe June will let me try a Camel if I promise not to tell. I'd tell Wolf, though. He'd never believe it.

I just can't believe June. She acts like a grown-up. As if she didn't have to ask anybody about anything. I wonder what that feels like. "I'm going in the house now and I'm going to read for the next year and nobody can stop me." Wow. June must feel like that all the time.

I've finished my cotton candy and I throw the paper cone into the trash can at the entrance to the Arcade. My mother and father and Wolf are standing with June and her parents down by the dock. My father is looking up to where I am and he calls out, "Down here, honey. Come on, we have to get back." He looks clean and fresh in his yellow summer shirt and tan shorts. I'm so glad he's my father I want to run up to him and hug him around the waist. I don't though. I just hurry down to the pier and climb into the canoe without saying anything to June or to anybody. I want to be back at the camp, in my bunk bed with Wolf sleeping above me in the dark.

That night I hear my mother and father talking outside the trailer. Their voices are soft but they are right under the little window across from the bunks and I can hear every word. They probably think we're asleep.

"He's as crooked as a damned corkscrew," my father says.

"I thought he was a friend of yours," my mother says. "Some way to talk about a friend."

"He's just one of the guys at the shop. I've known him for a couple of years but we've never even had a beer together."

"I don't like him. She seems okay. Timid little thing. Probably afraid of him, he's so big and kinda rough. He just doesn't seem right to me," my mother says.

They're talking about June's parents. I know it and it scares me. What's wrong with her father? How awful to have a father people talk about that way.

"Oh, he's not that bad. Just into every damned kind of deal you can imagine. New cars, new guns, fur coat for the wife and all on what I make or maybe a few bucks more a month. Can't be done legit, you know what I mean? Always looking for a way to outfox everybody. Wouldn't be surprised if he didn't do some time behind bars. Maybe has already." My father laughs but my mother is quiet.

"I'd worry about his wife and June. What kind of way is that for a man to act? He's a man with responsibilities. I don't see how that's funny."

I hear them move away from the window and everything is quiet. I want to go to sleep. To get away from my father's voice telling about June's father. But I can't sleep. All that money in her change purse. It didn't sound like her father is a bank robber or anything. Just crooked as a corkscrew. Poor June.

The next day starts out regular. We all go for a swim after breakfast and then Wolf and my father and I play catch while my mother straightens up the tent and the trailer. She says I should play in the sun and not bother to help her, so, as much as I hate to play ball, I stand way out in the field where all I have to do is chase the balls Wolf misses. He's a good ball player so I have an easy morning watching the bees bumble around the buttercups and bluettes growing in the dry grass and looking out to the lake. By lunch time I feel sunburned and the skin on my face is stiff.

"You've had enough sun, honey. Why don't you go over and see if June wants to play this afternoon? You two could do something quiet in the shade," my mother says.

She and I are picking up the paper plates and napkins from lunch and throwing them onto the coals of our fire. They just sit there for a minute right on top of the red hot coals and it looks like they won't burn and then all of a sudden they burst into flame and they're gone. It's a great way to do dishes.

"Okay," I say.

Finally, my mother thinks I've had enough sun and enough fresh air. Yay. I've been thinking about June since last night. I don't know how I feel about her. Maybe she's not so bad. And I'm sorry her father isn't quite right like my mother said. Anyway, I want to see that tent she was bragging about. I'll bet she's right. I'll bet it's a lot better than ours.

I walk through the long grass to where the trees start and cut through the woods on the path my father showed me. June's camp site is right on the other side of the woods. Not very far. Their field is back from the edge of the lake but there are three tall trees that give some shade to their tent. Wow, that is a big tent. I have never seen one that big. I walk slowly across the field. I'm kind of scared. I don't really know June's mother and father. What if they don't want me coming around. What if they're taking a nap or something. Maybe this wasn't such a good idea. I turn to walk back through the pine trees when I hear June's voice.

"Hey, where you going? Come on in. Nobody's home but me. Come on," she calls.

I turn back and walk over to the tent where she's standing, holding the flap open.

"Hi. My mother said maybe we could play together for a while. If you want to. If your parents don't mind," I say, standing just inside the tent, looking around at what looks like a real house. There's a real rug on the floor. And it is a floor. Big sheets of wood spread out over the dirt so you feel like you're in a house. And a stove with a pipe going up out of the top of the tent. There's a regular table in the middle of the room and regular chairs around in different places.

"You sleep in a real bed," I say.

"It's a cot, but it doesn't look like one. It has a real mattress," she says, sitting down on her bed.

Her parents' beds are on the other side of the tent. They have bedspreads on them. Not like a camp at all.

"Sit down," she says, pulling a straight chair close to her

bed with her foot and pointing to it. "Sit down and we'll have a smoke."
I can't believe she said that. A smoke. She must be joking. I sit down and look around some more. Everything is really nice but it's not clean like our camp. My mother keeps our tent and the trailer really clean. This place looks like gypsys live here. That's what my mother would say. "Only gypsys could live in this mess," she says when Wolf and I don't clean up our room. There are clothes lying all over the place and not just June's either. There's a cereal box on the floor near the stove. I'd never get away with that. And there are candy wrappers on the floor under June's bed. Baby Ruth and Walnettos and Hershey's. What a mess. I look away quickly so June won't think I'm spying on her.
June takes the silver cigarette case from the Arcade out of her pocket and clicks it open. She holds it out to me and I see there are five cigarettes in it, all in a row, held in by the silver clip. She isn't joking. What'll I do? I can't smoke a cigarette, for gosh sakes. And I can't not smoke a cigarette.
"What if your parents catch us?" I say, wishing they'd come into the tent that minute.
"They're gone for the day. They went back into town for something. Shopping, I guess. I don't know. Here, light up," she says pushing the case at me.
I reach over and lift up the clip. I take a cigarette with my thumb and first finger and then I look over to see what June is doing with her cigarette. All the while I'm thinking, her parents are gone for the day. They leave June all alone for the whole day. I love the idea of being alone all day. I would read and eat and eat and read and Wolf would have to fend for himself. Grandma Wolfson says that. 'You just have to learn to fend for yourself.' I'd be glad to fend for myself all day.
"Here's a light," June says, scratching a kitchen match on the bottom of her shoe. My father does that when he lights our camp fire. I've never seen a kid do it before.

I hold the cigarette the way they do in the movies, between the tips of my first and second fingers. I see June tap the end of her cigarette with her thumb so I do that too. Now she is holding the match to the end of my cigarette.

"Suck in," she says and I do.

Oh, gosh, my mouth is filled with hot smoke and I am coughing and coughing and my eyes are running and I can't get my breath.

"You're okay. Just breath in fresh air. You sucked in too fast. Do it slow, like this," she says and pulls smoke into her mouth through her cigarette. The lit end glows hot and I think she'll cough like I did. She doesn't though. She just blows the smoke out through her teeth like Joan Crawford and she doesn't cough at all. It looks so easy the way June does it.

My cigarette is lit so I try again, slowly. This time I think I will really die. I can't breath at all. I can't even cough. I'm choking. June gets up and slaps me on the back as hard as she can. I catch my breath but my eyes are still running tears down both cheeks and onto my shirt. I look for a place to put the cigarette but there is no ashtray or wastebasket or anything in sight. I drop it on the floor and June scrubs it out with the tip of her shoe. I feel bad to leave it there but she just shrugs her shoulders as if it's okay.

"I guess you're not a smoker," she says, smoke coming out of her mouth every time she says a word. "We can do something else."

June goes to the dining table and sits in one of the chairs. She just sits there without saying anything more, smoking and flicking her ashes on the floor. We sit like that for what feels like forever and then June says, "Want to go over to the general store?"

'Yes,' I say to myself. Of course I want to go across the road to the general store, but I don't answer June right away. The taste of the Camel is very strong on my tongue and I'm sure my breath smells of tobacco. I don't dare do another thing that my mother and father would be angry about, as much as I want to go with June.

"I better go home," I say.

"Okay," she says. She doesn't come to the tent flap with me but she calls out, "Come on back one day and we'll go for a swim."

I wonder why she made me promise not to tell about the cigarettes when we were at the Arcade. She doesn't act like her parents care one way or the other.

It's Friday of my father's vacation week. Monday morning he'll be gone. I'll miss him, but he'll be back for the weekends. Sometimes he comes just for supper and a swim after work. Then he spends the night and leaves before any of us are up in the morning so he won't be late to work. He says he's very lucky to have a job at the Tool and Die and he can't take any chances what with the depression being so bad. This morning he looks sad or worried, I can't tell which.

"Were you going over to play with June today, Pumpkin?" he asks.

We're standing on the dock skipping stones into the lake. My father's stones go very far out. They jump so many times I lose count. Mine hop once and sink, making ripples that come right up to the dock. Wolf is playing with his dump truck in the dirt near the trailer and my mother is making cornbread over the open fire for our breakfast so my father and I are alone. I love to be alone with him. He looks right into my eyes when he talks to me when we're alone. The rest of the time he and my mother talk into the air over our heads.

"I guess so. We didn't play yesterday, but she said maybe we'd take a swim off their dock together one day," I say.

"June and her family aren't there, honey. They've gone," he says sitting on the end of the dock and patting the place beside him for me to sit.

"Gone?" I say. What does he mean, gone? How could they be gone?

"Mr. Wilson lost his job at the Tool and Die and they're going to go out to Ohio where his brother has a farm. I know

June was sorry not to say goodby to you, but they had to get on the road early this morning. It's a long trip to Ohio," he says.

He has turned away from me and he's looking out over the water like he's trying to see something he lost on the other side of the lake. "These are hard times," he says and pats my knee. He does know I'm here. I try to think what it must be like for June, just leaving like that, but I'm thinking more about my father than I am about June. He seems so sad that it makes me want to cry. I don't, though and Daddy and I sit there on the dock not saying anything until my mother calls us for breakfast. We don't talk about June or her parents any more.

We're back home. The first week of school is over and so is my birthday. I got a diary for my eleventh birthday. It's from Grandma Wolfson and it has a key. "Just in case you don't want your thoughts known to little eyes," she said when I unwrapped it. She smiled at Wolf when she said it and I thought, 'If Wolf wants to read my diary he'll figure out a way to do it' but I didn't say it.

I've been writing some about last summer. Not everything, just what I think is important to remember. Like the day my father told me about June going away. I heard him talking to my mother after breakfast when I was down in the hammock.

"I was right," he said. "Wilson's in some kind of jam with the law. It's all over the shop. Stolen goods. Stuff from the shop, too, I guess. I feel sorry for his wife and kid."

"The poor things. Anything we can do?" my mother asked.

"No, they're long gone by now. Took their clothes and not much else. He's running as fast as he can run and there isn't too much room in that Pontiac of his. Suitcases and his family. Poor sucker," my father said.

He had lied to me about June but I was glad in a way. The things he told my mother were too sad and scary and I pretended that June was really on her way to a nice farm in Ohio

A few days later I got up the nerve to walk over to their campsite. The tent was there and I went over and lifted up the flap. The hairs on my arms stood up straight and my stomach was in a cramp I was so scared, but I decided that Jo March would have had a look around and that's what I did. I had a look around. The tent was messier than when I had visited June. Things were just dumped all over the place. It didn't look like they could have taken very much with them. There was a loaf of bread just sitting out on the table, open for the mice to eat. Raccoons, too, I bet. And coffee grounds spilled all over the beautiful rug. How could they leave that rug? All those beautiful things just left, like trash. I saw something shiny at the edge of the rug and went over to see what it was. It was the silver cigarette case, dented like somebody had stepped on it, but perfect otherwise. I picked it up and put it in my pocket. I would keep it for June, I decided. If I ever saw her again I would give her her cigarette case. She'd like that.

The rest of the summer was fine. I thought about June sometimes, but the camping part was much better than it had ever been. I read "Eight Cousins" and "Swiss Family Robinson", which I loved and "Tom Sawyer" which I didn't like all that much. Reminded me of Wolf, I guess. Our cousin Annie came to stay for a week in August. She's two years older than I am and she's fun. She taught me how to do a swan dive off the raft out in the lake and she went with me when I bought the vase at the Arcade. I was right about that. It fit into my hand like it had always been mine. I couldn't eat the cotton candy we bought, though. Too sweet. I gave mine to Wolf. He never got the knife he wanted out of the steam shovel machine, but he says he'll get it for sure next year.

I keep the vase on the dressing table my father built for me. Wolf and I share our bedroom so I had to threaten him with death if he touches my vase. The silver cigarette case is under my hankies at the back of the drawer in the dressing table. Nobody ever goes in there but me.

THE TRAIN TO PARIS

at an Alpine station
on the train from Venice to Paris
we are roused from somnolence
by two border guards
and an Alsatian shepherd
you sit chin in hand at the window
dreaming of the Alps
I sleep stretched on the opposite seat
trying to lose an Italian cold and fever
before our days in Paris
the guards push the compartment door open
and in French bid the dog sniff out our contraband
his black wet nose is intimate and rude
and thorough
we are cowed
surprised speechless
and feeling somehow guilty
in seconds the dog retreats
prizeless but having done his job
the guards
without acknowledgement
back into the corridor
thrust open the door to the next compartment
we stare at one another for a time
finally you say
looking for drugs, I guess
it strikes us as a joke
we giggle
there is at the edge of our embarassed laughter
the uneasy knowledge that the dog is often successful
we feel a kind of pride in our innocent participation
in the dramatic daily doings
on the train from Venice to Paris

THE POEM ABOUT THE TRAIN TO PARIS

the poem about the train to Paris
is finished at least for now
I go to the telephone to share it with you
to be with you in the way we know how to use the telephone
no space between
love as close as breath
I punch in your number
wishing for the old dial
the intimate click click
my fingers find the numbered buttons
by now genetic information
the first ring
and the second
she isn't home
she's out of town till Tuesday
the thought is premonition
preparation
for the time when what we share
will have more than miles to travel
and will have to be closer than breath

BURGESS SHALE

On having read Stephen Jay Gould's "Wonderful Life"

treelike, rooted
drinking earth waters by osmosis
barkskinned, Druidic
leaf tangled head bowed only to the wind
I raise my branchbent arms and budded fingers
    to the sun
        and dream of flying

or

one-celled, I float in primal ocean deeps
and never dream at all

or

bi-pedal female, omnivorous
fair skinned, dark eyed, warm blooded
fragile in my ecosystem
I dream
    ten thousand worlds

or

I am George Bailey

or

CARDIFF WALLS

Welsh slate handset
contrariwise
on end snugged up to one another
friction and pressure
antigravity
dry walls and levees stand
gray black in rain

impervious unsettling
against the seam and nature of the rock
art and incantation
order imposed
for the time being

ANDREA DORIA

looks like a plate
it is a plate

no gurgle only static
words through water

short wave voice
in our Nantucket kitchen

drowned plate
recovered

call my wife
tell her I'll be home for supper

THE LESSON

off balance about to fall
    face down into the stars
we learn we certainly learn
    reaching for fingerholds in air
    toe dancing on the ether
    forward pressure in the small of the back
we learn we certainly learn
    to breathe a vacuum
    to walk upon the void
    to eat the dust of galaxies
    and to prevail

HEAD OF THE TABLE

Memoir

We were nomads. It was the Depression of the thirties and we moved time and again to where Dad could find work. Mom made each new place home within minutes of our unpacking. The house in Holland, Michigan, the apartment in East Hartford, Connecticut, the house in Greenfield, Massachusettes, and all the others, were familiar to my younger brother, Todd, and me as soon as the beds were made and supper was on the table.

Mom was a good match for Dad in most things. She was adaptable, clever at stretching the household money, bright, and ready for adventure. And she was madly in love with him.

Dad's love for her was exceeded by his need for her nurturing. He was a creative, exciting, difficult man, gifted and ego-centric. He was a pilot in the days when they were still called aviators and when they were regarded with the same awe that was otherwise reserved for movie stars. His pilot's licence bears the blue ink facsimile signature of Orville Wright and the date 1926. He was an inventor, an amateur musician and actor, and the designer and builder of an eponymous low wing monoplane, the Williams Monoplane. He was also an asthmatic and, as the result of a childhood farm accident, an amputee. He wore a heavy wood and leather leg where his own had been. Snapshots of him show a smiling, smartly dressed young man, looking like an F. Scott Fitzgerald character in argyle vest and tweeds. I remember him that way. And there are other memories. Dad, sitting up in his bed, pillows propped behind him, an oxygen tent spread above and around him, his face ashy pale and covered with sweat. I hear him dragging breath into his lungs. I hold my own breath until I hear him breath out and in again.

"Kids! Todd, Shirley, come into our bedroom when you get your pyjamas on," Mom calls.

We are in Glastonbury, Connecticut. We are upstairs in the Cape Cod house Dad had built for us a year and a half ago. We live here by ourselves, Mom, Dad, Todd and I. No uncles, aunts, friends, as there have been at other times. Just the four of us. I am eleven and I have my own bedroom for the first time since I was two and a half. It is one of those perfect times that we assume will last forever when we are children.

Todd and I sit on the floor at the foot of our parents' bed. Dad has been in bed all day with an asthmatic attack. Mom is sitting beside him on the bed, rubbing his back. They both look serious and I feel a shiver of anxiety as I tuck my bathrobe around my feet and glance over at my brother. He is pushing a toy car back and forth on the bedroom rug and seems unaware of the tension in the room.

"Daddy and I have been talking. He isn't doing very well here in Connecticut, you know. His asthma, I mean. The dampness is bad for him."

Dad doesn't talk. It's all he can do to breath.

"We've been thinking about going to live somewhere where he can be more comfortable. Well, that's the fun part," Mom says, her voice artificially light. She isn't fooling me. She hates this, but I'll go along. She is taking us in on something momentous. No one has ever discussed anything serious, a grown-up thing, with us in just this way before. I have a growing feeling of responsibility and power as she speaks.

She speaks and then is quiet. A little bit of news at a time. Long moments for Todd and me to take it in, digest it, understand what she means. I understand in a flash. We're moving again. I'll have to leave my beautiful bedroom. For the first time, the news of a move is devastating to me. Not adventure this time, but the awful business of keeping Daddy alive.

"Where?" I say, finally.

"What's the fun part, Mom? Where are we going?"

"Not only where, but how," she says, leaving Dad and coming to sit with us on the floor. Now she really looks excited. Maybe this won't be so bad.

"We're going to take the trailer Dad built and travel to California in it!"

Todd stops rolling his toy car, looks up at her and says, "The trailer! Great!" At eight, he is more interested in rolling stock than in our destination or the reason for the trip.

"We'll leave at the end of May and take a nice long time, as long as we want. We can see the country. Indians and mountains and the Grand Canyon. We'll have a wonderful vacation."

"Indians. Swell," Todd says, sitting up and looking interested at last.

"But where, Mom? Where will we live?" I need the particulars to help me deal with the sudden cramping in my stomach. I will be in seventh grade in September and I really want to be with my friends. So many Septembers have found Todd and me in new schools with strangers that the transition to Junior High has become exceptionally important to me. Please let me be with Betty and Dotty, I think, knowing that that is not a possibility. The grown-up feeling is dissolving and there are tears in my throat.

"Near Hollywood. Burbank is the name of the city. Aunt Mildred and Uncle Charles live in North Hollywood, remember? And Phyllis? You'll have Phyllis out there to play with. Mildred found us a nice house with a date tree in the yard. What do you think of that?"

"It'll be fun," Dad says, the air wheezing through his open mouth.

Fun. In spite of everything, he meant it. All these years later, I know they both meant it. It would be an adventure. And so it was. We saw our Indians and we marveled at the Grand Canyon and we were properly awed by the Rockies. Our first stop in California was at a roadside stand for huge glasses of fresh orange juice, a celebration of our arrival. Our house was small and Todd and I were sharing a bedroom again. And for the first time since he was in kindergarten, we were not going to the same school. We all made our adjustments. Dad's was the hardest. He could no longer fly. His health was too bad. At thirty-six, he had to take a job in a factory, Lockheed Aircraft. It was 1939 and the industry was revving up. We would all be flying everywhere in the new air age. And there was the likelihood of war.

"Which way does Toddy come home from school? Quickly, Shirley, I have to get him home."

Uncle Charles is standing at the curb in front of our bungalow when I come home from school. He looks worried and he's nearly shouting at me. I am frightened so suddenly that I can't remember which way Todd comes home. At that moment I see him ambling toward us, stopping to pick up something from the sidewalk as he goes. A stone, a bit of glass, his pockets are full of his treasures.

"There he is," I point and rush away into the house, to Mom. Away from whatever it is that Uncle Charles is going to tell us.

"Mom? Where are you, Mom?" My voice is thin and I'm sure she can't hear me, even in this tiny house.

"Here, dear. In the bedroom. Come in quietly, honey. Daddy's sleeping."

Daddy's sleeping? It's three-thirty in the afternoon. He must have had an asthma attack.

I enter my parents' bedroom and I have to wait for my eyes to adjust to the dim light after the bright California sun outside before I can see that there are two strangers standing by the bed. My mother is sitting on the edge of the bed, holding Dad's hand, which lies limp on the light blanket.

"The doctor and nurse are here to help your Daddy. He's having a very hard time of it. This is our daughter, Shirley," she says to the two dark figures, both of whom are stepping back from the bed, making room for me beside my father.

Mom says, "Come closer, dear. You can talk to him, but I'm not sure he'll answer you."

The oxygen tent has been lifted so I can get close to my father. Todd comes into the room and joins me on the bed. No one has said that Dad is dying, but I know it. He is already so far away and I can't think of anything to say that will bring him back.

"I love you, Daddy," I say. I poke my brother and say, "Tell him you love him."

We kiss our father's cool, damp cheek and go into the living room to sit with our aunt and uncle until late afternoon.

"Does this mean I can't go to the movies?" Todd asks.

"Of course you can't, stupid," I say, outraged. I am twelve and I have no patience for a nine-year-old.

"We'll have to go home," I say, thinking of the comfort of my room in the Cape Cod house with longing. Everything will be fine when we get back there.

At seven thirty, when Dad's sheet covered body has been carried from the bedroom, through the living room and out of the house, Mom says, "We must give these good people some supper. Can you get something, Shirley?"

Aunt Mildred and Uncle Charles have left, promising to be here first thing in the morning. Mom must mean the doctor and the nurse, who have been here since just after I left for school and have eaten nothing all day. Mom's asking me to fix some supper for all of us. I can do that. I want to do that. To be busy and needed and grown-up. I open three cans of Campbell Cream of Tomato Soup and make a stack of toast. Todd and Mom set the dining table and we all gather to eat this strange meal, the doctor on one side with Todd and the nurse on the other, next to my usual chair.

I start to sit in my chair, leaving Dad's place vacant, but Mom says, "Take Daddy's chair, Shirley. Please sit at the head of the table."

BROTHER

we're what's left you said
our morphine-dreaming mother having died
I know, I said
thinking
it means more to you than it does to me
being the remnant

the ego-centric world
before you came
when I was what there was
now that was something
I fail to see how
being two
an equal two
is worth remarking

it means more to you
I thought
because you only know a world with me in it

that was days and weeks and time ago
now I hear your voice or see your gray head from behind
and I think
we're what's left

clever of you to have known what that would mean

COWS

you girls see to the creatures
our grandmother calling
quaver voiced in August heat
she means bring in the cows
down driveway dirt to town paved road
shaded all the way
and smothering hot
we walk side by side
compatriots
equal in all things
look both ways
watchful for the sometime car
the possible Good Humor truck
no penny in our pockets but hope
and the still not dead belief in magic
cross the road to where the tall grass starts
Kate walks ahead, becomes the figure in the foreground
I heel and toe her footsteps
watch her back and try to disappear
I am afraid of cows
their heedless hooves
stained ivory millstone teeth
grind crush buttercups and bluets
grass
spittle
slathering
black eyes showing too much white
roll madly back in tossing head
they'll catch me out
crush foot in sucking soil
snag flesh on horn
Kate stands at the fence and whistles
two notes
just right

how does she know
they come dragging gravity under them in dripping teats
she lifts the bar and steps aside to let them through the gate
then lowers it again
I stand and watch, her acolyte
we walk back behind the cows
Kate talking softly calling names
Blossom Bossy Daisy
they have no names to me but beast
once in the barn they take themselves to stalls
they stand stupid flicking flies
waiting to be yoked and fed
slobbering water each from her private fountain
at last I can approach them hay in hand
offering food not friendship
they accept
they have their own priorities
the hired man clanks milk pails down the steps
hikes his stool under the near cow and begins to knead her teats
swish swish swish swish
the hard stream rings against the pail
and foams the rising milk
good girl good cow he says in Swedish
deflecting now the stream to the barn cat's mouth
she waiting at his knee in perfect expectation
all satisfied all harmonious
cobwebbed sun warm on straw scattered floor
Kate smiles and pets the cat
wild thing tame under her fingers how
I hurry up to open air and light
fearing the hay mow
and the stupid beasts
Kate says we are best friends, cousins
equal in all things
all things but cows I say

BATHROOM MIRROR

white enamel proscenium
transparent scrim used here
    in place of glass
behind the gauze
the secret theater of my life proceeds

someone the obverse of myself
is permanently cast in the lead
I am audience to her ingenue
    her wife
    her mother
and now this late in the action
we stare at each other across the footlights
the graying she
uncertain of her lines
the graying I
hoping for a surprise
    in the last act

MOTHER AT EIGHTY THREE

you scare me old lady
your need foreshadows mine
your loneliness
is a pocket of ice in my chest
it will be my loneliness
your frailty
makes my bones brittle
the old-tea color of your eyes
    awash with sudden tears
is the color of sorrow
and the fear that your tears may cause me
    to turn away
so potent are they
you do not whine
or question fate
at least out loud
at least in my company
you give me all you have of courage
of laughter
of shared memory
and love
in spite of all you stand on time's ramparts
waving a bright banner
signalling
I think
that onward is the only way to go
I follow you in fear
and in the presence of the known end
you scare me old lady
and you challenge me and give me heart
onward is the only way to go

DNA

my father died
young
protesting
and my mother said
you have your father's hands
his eyes
his smile
his temper
quick
hot
harsh and unforgiving
I grew in strength
I was his surrogate

my mother died
six months ago
at ninety-three
transcendent with morphine
and the knowledge

this morning
my bathroom mirror showed her eyes
and the bald spot at the right temple
where she combed her white curls forward

late in the day
I understand my DNA

CEREMONY

in pastel summer dresses
the benevolent matriarchy
sits at tea
white wicker chairs and table
gray in dense maple shade
the lifted pot flicks silver
the aunts pass translucent china cups and saucers
one to the other
in casual ceremony
ordinary as Communion
they do break bread, the celebrants
thin white bread buttered thinly
murmuring ritual words
lemon milk sugar

the comfortable sanctity
of this fellowship
assumes
a stained glass window
between initiates
and the rest of the world

AUGUST 1943

I walk behind the hay wagon
breathe dust motes
itch with what will be poison ivy by supper time
muscles lift phantom bales
remembering the heavy fork up down up down since breakfast
and no time for lunch
sun low over apple trees
our orchard where the bees know me
I am locked in step with the steaming horses
Old Tom who snaps at me
and Vulcan whom I ride in winter
we walk the grassy path to the barn
to shadowed dusk and food and rest
I imagine time is passing

STRING OF PEARLS

On Sunday
In the rainy afternoon
We danced
In the dining room
In the forty-first year of our marriage
We danced
In our joy
And in the intimate knowledge of death
We danced
In laughter and in love
We danced

MINE

A Story

"Wallace, it's on the table." Announcement. Warning. The unsaid 'come and get it or I'll feed it to the chickens' sounding in the blat of Esther's voice.

She doesn't expect him to appear. She knows where he is. In their bedroom at the back of the house, sitting straight up in the ladder back chair that was his grandmother's, that she never sits in because it's so uncomfortable, not a forgiving place in the seat or in the back. He's staring out the window in the direction of the barn, but she doesn't think he sees the stretch of dirt, the few chickens scratching at the dry, hard earth, the barn beyond. His eyes, faded from the sky blue they were when she met him, look unfocused a lot of the time.

"Waiting for rain, the Lord knows, and I doubt he'd recognize it if it came."

For the past year or so she's thought he might be getting senile, forgetting where he is sometimes, forgetting to feed the chickens. Nothing serious, just things that make her wonder. Annoy her. Make him undependable around the place.

Wallace Furnold had delivered fresh eggs and milk to the State Orphan Home where she had lived since she was

55

nine. Since her mother wandered off and her grandmother got tired of trying to feed and clothe the three grandchildren her various kids had managed to leave with her. Since the county came and took two of the grandkids off to foster homes and put Esther into protective care. "She's just so big and awkward. Hard to place." She didn't hate it at the home. She knew she was big and awkward, but the people there made nothing of it. They assigned her to the garden in spring and summer, digging up the old beds, forking in the manure, mulching. In the fall she raked leaves and in the winter she shoveled snow. The routine, the knowing when she got up in the morning exactly what would be expected of her, was soothing. It gave her time to herself without the screaming and the smacks on the head and the threats to 'give ya to the gypsies if they'll have ya', that had been the sound and the feel of her first nine years. Her feet in the ugly black oxfords, lady's size six, that she wore for the first year at the home, felt planted solidly in the dirt of the garden. The rough white sheets on her narrow bed smelled of bleach and were cleaner than any she had ever slept on. She would bury her nose in the coarse cotton and breath in safety and belonging as she fell asleep. The platters of vegetables, steamed limp and without butter or salt, that were passed along the plain wooden table in the dining hall suited Esther 'down to the ground'. She wasn't used to having meat in her diet so she didn't miss it. She ate the Sunday boiled chicken with boiled potatoes and boiled carrots, but it was the Dixie Cup of vanilla ice cream that followed that she waited for all week. One of the other children, a small girl with watery eyes and short, red curls named Grace, would trade her Dixie Cup for some of Esther's chicken. She had no words for how she felt about Grace, but if anyone, including supervisors or aides, spoke sharply to her, Esther was on them in a rage, shrieking and clawing. She was so big, so threatening to the untrained, ill-paid aides, that Mrs. Appel, the head supervisor, would have to step in. She would send Esther to the store room, which Mrs. Appel called the 'quiet room', where she could think on her "wild temper which will have to be curbed if you are to enter polite society when your stay with us comes to an end". Esther enjoyed the time alone in the small space off the dining hall.

'I'll have a garden of my own', she would think, sitting on a low stool in the far corner of the windowless room. 'I'll bake pies and make apple sauce and sew pretty dresses for myself. And I won't have anybody else in my house. Just me.'

When Esther was eleven Grace was adopted. One gray winter day, a Friday after school classes were over and just before time to wash up for dinner, Mrs. Appel came into the large room where classes were held and rapped on the blackboard with a piece of chalk.

"Attention, everyone. I have some very good news for all of you. Quiet, please."

Esther had never before heard the phrase 'good news'. Her heart leapt in her chest. What on earth? Good news for all of us. Ice cream every day. No more school. Esther's imagination flagged.

"Our Grace has been chosen by a wonderful couple with two children of their own. She has been adopted. She leaves us today. There is hope for every one of you. Isn't that good news?"

Grace, standing quietly beside Mrs. Appel in a new blue coat and hat, sucked her thumb and looked down at her new patent leather shoes. Esther stared at Grace and tried to think what it all meant. No more Grace. No one she cared anything about in the world. 'You have to be really careful of good news,' she thought.

"Wallace, you in there?" She knows he is but she wants him to know she's coming as she walks to the bedroom door. Give him a chance to get up out of his chair and come in for supper. A chance to act normal for once.

Her time at the home, her life after Grace, became one time. She didn't think of separate days or hours. There were changes. To chicken on Sunday was added meat loaf on Wednesday and finally, two weeks before she left, hot dogs for lunch on Saturday. She knew that the home had been visited by representatives of the State and that Mrs. Appel's successor, Mr. Fielding, had been told to add protein to the diet of the children in his charge, but it made little difference to her. Meat of any kind made her feel bloated and unwell and she tried not to eat the little that was put on her plate. The changes in what was offered at dinner became one with everything else. Children came and went. Aides and supervisors came and went. The seasons changed and she did whatever seasonal job was required of her without complaint. She had no more tantrums.

There were no mirrors in the home with the exception of the wavy, blotched glass above the sinks in the bathroom so Esther had only the slightest idea of what she looked like. She had had to bend to see into the mirror to comb her hair since she was ten. It was not a secret that she was the tallest girl in her grade. In the next three grades. By the time she was seventeen she was six feet one inch. After that she stopped growing but it was too late for her to get control over her limbs by that time. She moved like a mis-strung puppet. What she thought of as careful, lady-like gestures were seen as laughable, stuck-up attempts to fit in with her more delicate classmates. The two words she overheard the aides use when they talked about her were the familiar *gawky* and *awkward*. 'Just a pure statement of fact', she thought. Her hair was black and straight and very thick. Mrs. Appel had had it cut in what she called a Dutch Bob but with no bangs and as a consequence a piece of it always fell across her forehead and into her eyes. She had no bobby pins or barrettes and was constantly throwing her head back, like a stallion, clearing her eyes of that lock of hair. The others called her *Indian* or *Apache* because of her black hair. She paid no attention to the names and would answer only to Esther. Her eyes, small and dark, squinted back at her from the distorted glass. The light from the single ceiling hung bulb cast shadows on the permanent smudges under her eyes and made her look sick even to herself. Her full, loose lips showed strawberry red on the damp inner surface and blue on the outside, like raw beef exposed to air. She rejected her reflection as too dark, too large and looming. Threatening, almost. She knew that what she saw was Esther, was the person others saw when they looked at her, but it was not who she was. She was tall, yes, but thin boned, not quite fragile. She had brown eyes, yes, but they were large and wide set, open to the world. She was a girl, soon to be a woman, who moved through the space around her with grace and delicacy. She was not *Indian* or *Apache* nor even *Esther*. The girl she knew she was had no name except *myself*.

    She stops and bends to straighten the small floral rug that is the only bright spot in this room that serves as living room, dining room and kitchen. The only bright spot except for Esther's plants on the sills of the two windows on the south-east side of the house. There she grows African violets and staphalocarpus and Boston ivy which she is training to grow on twine she has strung up the sides of the window frames in lieu of curtains. The paper shades at these windows are yellow with age and torn at the bottom where the pulls have come off. She keeps them raised as high as she can and is trying to decide whether to get rid of them. If the ivy fills in she'll throw the shades in the trash or burn them in the wood stove. On her way to roust Wallace she stops again and tweaks a dead white blossom off the staphlocarpus. There are six buds waiting to bloom. 'A very satisfactory plant', she always thinks. 'You know where you are with plants.'
    "I'm coming in there, Wallace Furnold. Get your butt up off that chair."

She was used to seeing Wallace drive up the long approach to the home in his old black Ford pick-up. Didn't give him a thought, really, for years. And then she was seventeen and the day when she would have to leave, go out and find a job and live in a rooming house or somewhere, was only a couple of months away. She was in the kitchen scrubbing sheets against a scrub board in a big wooden tub, her hair hanging over her eyes, her knuckles red and swollen with the hot water, when he spoke to her.

"Name's Wallace Furnold. I farm out by the reservior. Got five acres and a good barn. I been married. Rose. She died four years ago. Mr. Fielding tells me you're gonna have to leave here soon. You want to come out to the farm? You want to get married? I'd treat ya decent."

She had looked up then, dried her hands on the towel tucked into her waistband, stepped back from the washtub and looked at Wallace Furnold without speaking. She saw an average looking man, average coloring, average height. As much as she could tell, anyway, not having seen many men to grade him by. His eyes were blue, his hair a mix of light brown and gray. His hands, hanging at his sides neither limp nor stiff, looked small and clean. His overalls were washed and his boots were old and scuffed, but not muddy. He knew enough to scrape his boots before coming into anybody's kitchen. She didn't think 'What does he want with a big old clod like me?'. She thought, 'A house and a barn and a garden. If I have to take a husband to get all that, this one doesn't look too bad. A farm's better than a rooming house.'

They were married at the home on her eighteenth birthday, her last day as an official orphan and ward of the state, she in a navy blue cotton dress and navy oxfords out of the donation box from the Baptist church, he in a clean pair of chinos, a tan work shirt, and a tweed jacket. She had no flowers and didn't miss them. Expectation had been damped in her like a coal fire, not quite extinguished but lending no warmth.

The wedding night was no worse and no better than she had thought it might be. She had some idea of what to expect from watching the farm animals and from what little her mother had told her before she abandoned her. "Men stick it in ya and ya get a baby." Wallace, who slept in his long johns, had poked what he called his pecker out of the flap of grayish white cotton knit, climbed on top of her and inserted the thin finger of flesh into what the matron at the home had called her 'privates' and for which she herself had no name. He had pumped a couple of times, penetrated, gasped a bit and withdrawn, all in the space of a minute or two. It had hurt only a little and she had turned on her side and gone to sleep. She had thought that she would be pregnant and waited for signs of a coming baby for the next few weeks. When none came she put it out of her mind. It did not occur to her to ask Wallace why he thought there had been no baby. His demands on her were infrequent, a few times a year and then not insistent. If she had said 'no' he would have turned his back and slept with no word of reproach. She knew this about him and she never said 'no'. But each time she spent a few days hoping she would quicken, like the single cow they kept for milk and butter who calved every other year as easily as she gave milk and whose calves were sold as soon as weaned and were never named. The years passed, they remained childless and she stopped giving the possibility a thought. What she had gained by marrying Wallace, her garden, the chickens, the small house, filled her days.

'Mine,' she would think, scrubbing the rough floor on her hands and knees. Not 'ours'. Not hers and Wallace's, but hers alone. "My rug needs beating," she would say. She would hang the bright bit of floral wool over the clothes line Wallace had strung for her between the two beeches that shaded the side yard. Then she would carry the wire rug beater with her to the yard, black wire twisted into flat curlicues and secured to a wooden handle. The beater and the rug had belonged to Wallace's mother he told her, the rug hand hooked by her from scraps of wool from his father's old shirts. She took great care not to beat too long or too hard, but to let the spring air freshen the roses and the exotic, unnamed blossoms his mother had invented for her rug. She was mindful of the fact that another woman had created it but the rug was hers. 'My windows need washing' or 'My blankets need to be rebound'. She never said these things out loud. Not for any sensitivity for Wallace's feelings. They just didn't talk much. He tended to the barn, the cow, feeding the chickens. She would have liked to strew the chicken feed, clucking the way Wallace did, low in his throat, to call them to their food, but he never brought it up. Their tasks were their tasks. He didn't interfere with the way she ran the house or the way she cooked and she didn't remark on his performance of his duties. The years went by without friction and without any growing closeness between them.

He mentioned his first wife, Rose, only once. "I don't have no Christmas tree. Rose didn't hold with pagan trappin's." She had not expected a tree or a present so she felt no loss and did not resent his mentioning his dead wife. There was little of Rose in the house; a crocheted antimacasser on the back of the one upholstered chair, a faded sepia print of Jesus in a dime store frame above their bed. Esther guessed that the tired, scraggy rose bush in a corner by the back stoop had been planted by Rose.

Wallace showed no interest in the flowers she spent so many hours cultivating, weeding, propagating in the cold bed she had made from a discarded window frame and four planks from a pile of wood in the dark interior of the barn. She'd have been embarrassed if he'd commented on them. Besides they were her flowers. Nothing to do with him.

Esther says her rote prayers every night, the prayers taught her by the minister who visited the home three times a year to see to the souls of 'the poor dear little creatures'. Not "Now I lay me down to sleep" but "Thank you, God, for all the gifts we have received from Thy loving servants. We will live to glorify Thy name. Amen." For the last few years she has added, "Thank You for the farm and for the flowers and for my house." She has nothing she would call faith but she does not want to take a chance on losing what she has gained. If a prayer will protect her world she prays it fervently. Lately there has been a feeling close to panic that rises in her chest just before she sleeps. She knows she has become cross with Wallace in the past months. She hears the strident tone of her own voice and doesn't know how to sound like her old self.

'He pays me no mind unless I scold,' she thinks, excusing herself, putting off the knowledge that there has been a change in him that is deeper than a lack of attention to her requests that he come to dinner, that he bring a ten pound sack of flour when he goes into town. His preoccupation with what he sees as drought annoys her. There is no lack of rain in her world. Her flowers, even Rose's rose bush, are healthy and blooming. They have had what showers they needed all summer long and yet Wallace sits for hours at the bedroom window conjuring rain.

"We'll lose it all. Nothin' can live without water. There's a cloud, just there over the barn. See it? It'll bring rain by night."

It doesn't and he lies in bed, his back to her, his body rigid. Esther does not know how to get through to him. She says, "Wallace, you're a damn fool. We had a shower just last Thursday. More than we needed. Your whinin's drivin' me crazy."

He does not acknowledge her. She has stopped going into their bedroom except to sleep. She has begun feeding the chickens and milking the cow. He doesn't notice. She likes her new chores, likes the feeling of more of the farm being hers, but she is uneasy about Wallace. He has never been a strong presence in her life but now it seems to her he is fading entirely. Disappearing. The prospect of no Wallace at all is more troubling to her than she can admit.

She snaps at him because she cannot say to him, "I'm frightened, Wallace. You're leaving me and I don't want you to go." If she could say those words she would not be Esther. She would be a woman who cares about another human being, a woman who does not want to be an orphan, a ward of the state, an abandoned child, ever again. Somewhere in her night thoughts and in the moments with her zinnias, her stock, her snap dragons, she has an inkling, but it is not enough to stop her carping at him.

"There is no drought, you old fool and you're not carrying your weight around here. Get out and feed those poor chickens."

He shuffles through the house in his felt slippers but he doesn't make it to the back door, to the yard, to the barn. He stops at his chair, sits heavily, his one hundred and forty pounds settling in like three hundred, and he stares into the space of the kitchen, waiting for his next meal. If it isn't meal time, if an hour goes by and Esther has not placed his plate of meat loaf and gravy on the oil cloth covered table, he gets up and shuffles back to the bedroom. She wishes he would never leave that room. She can forget about him when he's out of sight, or almost, any way. She can go about her day, humming a fragment of a song she learned when she was still with her mother "You're the cream in my coffee, You're the salt in my stew" and feeling like everything is right, is normal. Then she hears his slippers on the wood floor of their bedroom and her spine stiffens, her fists clench and she thinks, "My God, here he comes again. What does he want from me?"

Today feels different to her. The asters are bigger and brighter than ever and she feels fall in the air. Winter will come and with it the added tasks of securing the barn, making sure the cow is cared for, milked and fed through the snow to come, fixing the loose shutter on the kitchen window, checking the roof shingles for possible leaks. All the things Wallace has always done and that both of them have taken for granted. She is strong and willing and the job will not be too much for her, taking Wallace's place. But it had been good to have another person moving through her days, thinking his own thoughts, doing what needed doing without asking her permission or advice. It has suited her. Today she knows that everything has changed. Her knees ache with the kneeling she has done, both in the garden and in the house, weeding and scrubbing. Her shoulders know that she has milked and lifted hay bales. She has never thought of herself as any particular age. She and Wallace have not celebrated birthdays, but she knows she is no longer young. Today, she knows it. Wallace is old and she is no longer young.

Esther walks into the bedroom, the sterile room she has shared with Wallace for what now seems like a long time. He is standing, looking out of the window at the lengthening shadows and the thin splotched sun of late afternoon. His shoulders sag in his worn tan cardigan and his trousers are baggy.

'He looks so helpless,' she thinks and her throat tightens. In all her life, in spite of all, she has never felt helpless. She has always known that whatever her reality she was big and strong and she could handle it. She knows she cannot handle this, Wallace's helplessness. And there's something else. She sees him as another person in the room. Not as a table or a kitchen chair. A person whose body sags in his sweater and whose trousers have grown loose.

"Look there, Rose. Good news. There's the rain," he says half turning to her.

"He thinks it's raining," she says, not caring that he calls her by his first wife's name.

She sees that he is crying, tears running down his face, landing on the window sill. Huge drops of water splashing on the coarse grain of the dry wood. She moves to him and puts her arms around his waist from behind, feeling his ribs, feeling his body heave with sobs. It is the first time she has touched him in day light.

'Mine,' she thinks.

"Rose, look," he says again, pointing to the round wet spots on the inside window sill. "Rain. We'll be all right."

She bows her head and surrenders her cheek to the rough wool of his sweater.

"We're fine, Wallace," she says.

THE ARCH

gravity of the stone arch
pulls at my spine
the keystone sitting as it does
on the back of my neck
just where the weight of my head
and the hang of my shoulders
meet
Atlas found this posture
this balancing of density on the nape
beneficial
it helped him get a purchase on the earth
over time
it doesn't do as much for me
my knees are buckling
the keystone drives me down
into the earth
Atlas found gravity bearable
it will bury me
arch or no arch

SPY

I am the spy among you
decoding unsent signals
reading what you haven't written
hearing what you leave unsaid
feeling touches where your fingers never were
I carry the gist of undreamt dreams
from here to there

the enemy pays me nothing
I work for the love of it

I am the mole among you
holding my flame to the invisible ink in which you write
bringing up the story of your life

not that one
you know
the one you hoped we'd never read

SAY SO

because we say so
power shifts
surmounts
or abdicates
is crowned or vanquished
by our leave

PARENTHESES

between parentheses
we draw a line
bisect it forever
looking for infinity
for hope that just before the close paren
there is an asterisk
a foot note
explication
arbitrarily we name each slice
this is a year and this a nanosecond
mortal
we seek to stretch the line
by halving it
naming what we cannot know
we die
chalk in hand
screaming for one more chance
to split the moment

NOT SACRIFICE

Not sacrifice
The word is over proud
It bleeds the courage from the act

But choice
In favor of the other
Is what moves the loving spirit

1933

THE CAR

A Story

The October day is Indian summer warm. Claire, buttoned into her heavy winter coat, is finding it hard to hurry uphill. She turned six in August and she knows the rules. When her mother says keep your coat buttoned she means it. There are lots of other rules, too. The one about not speaking to strangers. And not taking candy or gum from anybody you don't know. Her cotton undershirt and underpants are damp with sweat and her lisle stockings cling to her skin, but Claire will not unbutton her coat.

She is approaching Dr. Wilmot's house, still five long uphill blocks from home, when she feels the car beside her. She feels it slow and nearly stop right beside her. Only the curb between them. She makes herself walk faster.

'Go away, car. Go away. I can't look. I'm not supposed to talk to anybody in a car. Go away. Please, please, please, go away'

Turning to look at the car, acknowledging its presence, seems the same as speaking to the driver. The rule says nothing about looking at the car. 'Rules stop just when you need help,' she thinks. As she steps off the curb to cross

Cedar Street she risks a glance and catches the shine of the front fender, black, hard, inching along. She scuttles across the street and as she steps up to the sidewalk she hears a man's voice coming from the car. The voice sounds familiar. Who? Fred Cates?

"Hey, Claire, want a ride? I'm going right to your house. Taking some papers to your daddy. Come on, kiddo, we're almost there. Hop in."

A spasm of fear nearly makes her stop where she stands, too close to the curb, too close to the car.

'I wish I could go up on the lawn,' she thinks in panic.

There *is* a rule about that. About not trespassing on other people's property. Not even to get away from a strange car? She forces her feet forward against her terror. She turns her head for an instant to see who the driver might really be. Who is calling her, using her name, talking about her daddy, sounding like Fred Cates, driving Fred Cate's' car? How clever of him, whoever he is, to be able to sound so much like Fred Cates, her mommy's and daddy's friend, her friend. Fred Cates, who teaches at the boy's school in town, who has dinner with her family nearly every Sunday, who brings her Black Jack gum and once in a while that best of treats, a Hershey Bar.

"You shouldn't, Fred," her mother says, "you'll spoil her."

Then when Fred has gone home, she and her father talk about him.

"He can't afford to feed himself on what he makes, much less bring things for Claire. The divorce wiped him out."

'Divorce,' she thought when she overheard them. What is it, divorce? 'Wiped him out' sounds like he's been erased from the blackboard. But he's still here.

Grownup language makes Claire anxious. She is always scrambling after a meaning that runs ahead of her

Claire likes Fred Cates better than any of her parents' friends. The men, anyway. Most of them get loud and red-faced at her parents' parties. Grabbing her onto their fat laps and kissing her on her face and on her neck. She hates all of them. On the night of a party she hurries to bed and pretends to be asleep before the guests arrive. One or another of them will come to her bedroom door to 'see the little princess' and she buries her face in her pillow, wishing them away, praying for her mother to rescue her. Once in a while Claire hears her mother's voice from the living room or the kitchen.

"Let the child sleep. Come on back to the party."

But Frank or Aldo or Buddy never pays any attention to what her mother says. And her father never says a word to any of the men who visit her bedroom on party nights. On those nights when her parents' friends smell of something nasty, the way Daddy smells when he's had a glass of bathtub gin with his supper. She has no idea what that means, bathtub gin, but she knows the smell and the look and the sound of her father when he's drunk a glass of it and poured another and she hates it. Hates how loud it makes him. How nasty he is to her mother when he's had a couple of glasses of the clear liquid he pours from a Mason jar into a pitcher before he puts it on the dinner table. Mommy won't have the Mason jar on the table. She likes things nice she says at almost every meal.

Claire feels uncomfortable getting into her bath at night. Bathtub gin. What does it have to do with this white, chipped enamel place where she bathes? Where she plays with her toys and sometimes splashes her mother? She wishes she could go into the back yard and shower under the hose. Or take what her mother calls a cat bath at the kitchen sink. The feelings she has about the men, about the bathtub, aren't anything she can talk about with anyone. Fred Cates is no part of it. He comes to the parties, but he's always Fred Cates. Just the same. Friendly and happy. Never strange or loud or putting his hands on her.

Now she forces herself to walk faster, run a few steps and then walk. Anything to get away from the man in the big black car. The car that looks like Fred Cates' car. Daddy says

that real Fred is lucky to have his car. That it's about all he has left. That with the depression and all, he'd better hold onto it. It's likely to be the last car he'll have for a long while.
The depression. Claire can only guess at the meaning of words like divorce and depression. She knows they are 'in a depression'. Her parents use those words often, but they do not explain to Claire what that means. 'In a scary place,' she thinks. In trouble of some kind. But what kind of trouble? Is she in it, too? Sometimes she thinks it has to do with Daddy's job. More often she's sure it's about the food they eat, the clothes they wear. But what? Most of her clothes are nice. She hates her winter coat, but her skirts and dresses are pretty and they fit her. She always has good food to eat. A good lunch to take to school. Some of her friends have different lunches. Bread with bacon grease spread on it. When Billy Fox, who usually sits next to her at lunch, opens his brown paper bag, unwraps the waxed paper from around his white bread and drippings sandwich, the smell makes her weak with hunger, with appetite, with longing for Billy's lunch. Her mother will not give her a drippings sandwich. Won't even talk about it.

"It hasn't come to that yet, thank God," is her only answer when Claire asks.

Claire always has an apple for dessert. Few of the other children ever bring fruit. She thinks they don't like it. Sometimes, though, she gives her apple to Sally. Sally doesn't bring lunch from home. The teacher, Miss Brown, gives her graham crackers from the big box she keeps in the storage closet at the back of the room, the box she brings out at recess. For a penny you can buy a graham cracker. For two pennies you can get a small carton of milk. Miss Brown puts pennies in the box for those who forget to bring them. So Sally has graham crackers twice a day. Sally always thanks Claire when she gives her her apple.

Claire thinks Sally looks sad most of the time. But in the playground when they play Red Rover or tag and Sally wins, beats the boys, she laughs. Sally throws her head way back, her stringy brown hair flying, and she laughs to the skies. Claire loves to see her laugh. There is something dangerous about it. Claire is frightened for Sally, but pleased for herself. As if Sally were breaking rules for Claire in exchange for the apple

'I wish I was Sally right this minute,' Claire thinks desperately as she pushes her feet faster uphill, panting now and sweating from every pore, moving away from make-believe Fred Cates, away from unimaginable danger.

'If I were Sally I could just run as fast as the wind and be home before he could catch me.'

"Honey, its all right. It's me, Fred. Want a ride home?"

He's sounding even more like Fred. 'What can I do?' Fear makes her stumble on the sidewalk. Just when she's sure she'll fall, that he'll jump out, pick her up and put her in the trunk of the big black car, he pulls away, leaning over to the passenger window to call out to her, "Okay, fraidy cat. See you at your house." Laughing just like Fred Cates.

She watches the car pull ahead and another car come along Main Street behind it. And another and another, until she loses sight of it in the line of cars moving up the hill. She slows her steps and sucks in the warm air, trying to catch her breath. She clutches the book she has forgotten she is carrying. The *First Reader* Miss Brown has said they must take home and cover with brown paper. "To keep it fresh for the next child who uses it." Claire loves covering books with a cut up brown paper bag. It makes her feel competent, powerful, in the way that scrubbing the bathtub with Bon Ami on Saturday mornings does. Trusted to do the thing right.

Claire loves Miss Brown. On the first day of school she took Claire's hand and led her into the class room. She walked with her over to the desk that would be hers. Told her how pretty she looked in her new yellow cotton dress. And just this morning Miss Brown had complimented Claire on her crayon drawing, her picture of the lake her father had taken her to one warm Saturday last July. Her mother had been getting a permanent wave at the beauty shop. Mommy would be gone nearly all day, so her father had driven Claire up into the hills to see this beautiful lake. The two of them had walked along the shore under the trees, skipping stones on the glass surface of the water. Her daddy could skip seventeen times in a row. Claire's stones made a quick circle and sank, the circle widening, making other circles inside themselves, going how far, Claire wondered.

When Miss Brown had said "You may draw anything you like this morning," Claire had drawn the lake with the mountains around it and the trees along the shore. She thought it was the best picture she had ever done and Miss Brown had agreed. She had said, "You really captured the color of the water, Claire. Good work." Claire trusts Miss Brown, knows she can say anything to her. Almost anything. Ask a question and Miss Brown will answer her, hear her. The thought of Miss Brown, her large bosom softly covered by the plain brown dress she had worn today, eases Claire's mind. Comforts her. Now that the danger of the black car has passed, Claire begins to look forward to getting home, having a glass of milk, and starting on the cover for her *Reader*.

'It's so hot. I wish I could unbutton my coat,' she thinks.

But she will not undo the large mother of pearl buttons that close the front of her heavy brown wool coat. Every morning Mommy says, "Keep your coat buttoned, Claire. I don't want you catching cold."

The coat is warm enough for the North Pole, she thinks, for Eskimos. And the ugliest thing she's ever seen. Claire loves beautiful things. Things like her mother's blue velvet evening gown. Her only evening gown. She wears it at all their parties. Claire knows that if it were her dress she would wear it to every party, too.

Claire hates the coarse fabric of her coat, the rough feel of it against the flesh of her fingers, the back of her neck.

The coat was a gift from her Grandmother Fiske on Claire's sixth birthday. Grandma Fiske can be counted on to know what is closest to Claire's heart. She is her best friend in the world. She will, Claire is certain, give her a baby doll or a china tea set or a pair of ice skates. But the big white box with the blue ribbon tied in a huge bow had held not a baby doll, not a china tea set, and worst of all, not a pair of ice skates for going with her father to Horse Pond to learn to skate.

Claire had knelt on the living room rug, the white box in front of her, and untied the bow. Grandma Fiske's bows always untied. You didn't need scissors. Her grandmother had leaned forward in the wing chair, looking anxious, and whispered to Claire, "Not what you hoped for, my darling, but what you need. Sorry, Clara." Grandma Fiske calls her Clara after a little girl in one of the story books Claire loves to have her grandmother read aloud.

"Skates for Christmas, maybe. You can't skate in August anyway," she had said, trying to make Claire laugh. Claire had pushed aside the folds of white tissue paper, had seen a dark brown mound of fabric, four wooden buttons down the center. It was a coat.

'I don't need a winter coat in August either,' she had thought.

Claire had looked over to where her mother sat on the couch, hoping for deliverance, for her mother to change the coat into skates. Her mother had been silent. The look on her face, lips tight, eyes boring into Claire had said "Thank your grandmother properly, Miss." And she had. Had swallowed past the hope of a tea set or ice skates and had kissed her grandmother, who had hugged her and pressed her cheek to Claire's so hard that Claire had felt her grandmother's cheek bone through her flesh. It had seemed to Claire that there would be a bruise under her eye if she had looked in the mirror. Her mother had come to kneel across from her. She had lifted the coat from the box, shaken it out and held it up for Claire to see. Held it by the shoulders, the stiffness of the fabric keeping the shape of the coat as if someone were already wearing it. No give, no softness anywhere. Her mother had said, "A beautiful winter coat, Claire. Just what you need."

'This big ugly thing, just what I need,' Claire had thought, wondering what she had done wrong that her mother could think that this might please her.

Claire had put on the coat and walked around the living room, her mother and grandmother saying how well she looked. How her height was wonderful for wearing clothes. Claire is tall and thin for her age. She had wondered what that could have to do with wearing clothes, since she has to wear them in any case, even if she were short and fat. They had just been trying to make her like this hideous coat and she could not. She couldn't even manage the buttons by herself. 'They feel like stones', she had thought, 'hard and rough and too big for the button holes. It looks like a coat for a hobo.'

Claire loves the word 'hobo'. She says it as often as she can. "He looks like a hobo." "She eats like a hobo." "I think I'll be a hobo when I grow up." Not aloud, but to herself, often.

Sometimes grown men come to the back door of their house on Elm Street. They knock as if they don't really want to be heard. Her mother will go to the door and there will be a man standing on the little wooden porch, woolen cap or frayed fedora in hand. He will say something too softly for Claire, standing safely in the hall, to hear. She is wary of strangers, but curious about the back door men. The hobos.

Her mother will say to the man, "Wait there. I'll find something for you."

Then she'll open the ice box and take out the bits of meat left from last night's supper and make a sandwich. Or she'll heat a bit of the soup or stew she's making for tonight, open out a clean kitchen towel, place it on the small tray she uses to carry poached egg and toast to Claire when she's sick in bed, place the dish and a fork or spoon and a fresh napkin on it and carry it to the waiting man. If it's winter she'll tell the man to eat on the back porch and leave the dishes on the bench. If the weather is warm she'll say, "Sit out on the lawn. Enjoy the sun."

The men are always polite. They say "thank you" and "God bless you". Grandma Fiske says that they put a mark on the house so other hobos will know Mama is a softy. Claire loves to hear her mother called a softy. She thinks it means that Grandma knows special things about her mother, things Claire doesn't know but that make her happy.

Now, walking home in the Indian summer heat, Claire wishes she could give her coat to one of the ragged men who come to their door. Maybe one of them has a little girl who would really love it. As she walks, she fingers the bottom button, sliding it in and out of the button hole. The mother of pearl is slippery and she can manage to button and unbutton by herself. As soon as Grandma Fiske had left the house on Claire's birthday, her mother had gone to her button box. She had taken out four of the six white buttons that she had saved from her own blue spring coat when it had become too frayed to be of use to anyone. She had cut the ugly brown buttons from the front of Claire's coat and sewn the ugly white ones on in their place. Her mother had smiled at Claire as she held out the coat with its row of gleaming buttons. Claire had felt tears filling her eyes, had blinked them back and taken the coat from her mother's hands. 'It's worse,' she had thought, 'a thousand, million times worse'.

Why had Mommy done it? And seemed so happy about it. The coat makes her sad whenever she puts it on.

Now Claire begins scuffing through the dry leaves that have drifted over the sidewalk. She loves the smell of the dust she raises. She begins to feel easier. She will help Daddy rake the leaves in their yard on Saturday. He'll build a bonfire at the back of their lot and she will stand safely back and watch him feed the leaves into the fire, a careful rakeful at a time. They will stand together when the fire has died to ashes, seeing pictures in the embers, dragons and witches and castles.

She is thinking so hard about the bonfire, about standing in the early dusk, her hand in her father's hand, that she is surprised to find herself at her corner. Suddenly the terror is back. It turns her knees weak, makes her keep her eyes on the ground in front of her, afraid to look across the street to her house, third down on the left. Will the car be in front of her house? Does make-believe Fred Cates really know where she lives? Yes, the car is there at the curb, just the way Fred Cates always parks when he comes for dinner on Sundays.

As suddenly as it had come, the terror leaves.

"The bad Fred saw the real Fred's car and went away. Good I did the right thing. I was good. I didn't go with the bad Fred Cates. Mommy will be proud of me."

Claire switches her book to her left arm and skips along the walk at the side of their tan stucco house to the back porch. She goes into the kitchen, stops long enough to drop her books on the oil cloth covered table, unbuttons her coat, walks down the hall toward the front of the house. She can hear her mother's voice coming from the living room. And another voice. Fred Cates and her mother are laughing together. She walks toward the archway into the living room, keeping her footsteps quiet, hoping to surprise them. To tell them about her clever escape from make-believe Fred Cates.

"I couldn't trick her. She wasn't having anything to do with me. Wouldn't come near the car," Fred Cates was saying to her mother. It had been real Fred Cates, after all. How could she have known?

'He's talking about me,' Claire thinks, uncomfortable in a way she can't name.

"Isn't she the most serious child you ever saw? Afraid of her shadow sometimes. Wait till I tell Tommy. He'll die laughing," her mother answers, laughing.

Her mother and Fred Cates laughing. So it's funny that she wouldn't get into his car. Wouldn't take a ride home with him. Tears blind her. She's afraid she'll stumble. She creeps past the archway without being seen, reaches the stairs, tiptoes up and goes to her room. She lies on her bed, staring at the ceiling, tears running down her temples and into her hair, until she hears Fred Cates leave. Moments later she hears her father's voice in the hall. Now Mommy will tell him and Daddy will laugh. Sorrow makes it hard to breath normally. It sends the blood to her face and makes her body too heavy to move.

By the time her mother calls her down to supper she feels sick. She drags herself to the table where her parents are seated, waiting for her. Her mother serves her plate and her father passes the bread. Supper goes on as usual. Nobody notices that she is pushing the hash around on her plate and isn't eating a bite. Neither of her parents speak to her except to say, "Sit up straight, Claire," and "How was school?"

She says, "Good. We learned a new song."

They both say, "That's nice" at the same time, but they don't ask her what song or ask her to sing it. She couldn't sing now, anyway. She is glad they're treating her normally. Not asking her about the car. Maybe her mother has forgotten.

The following Sunday Fred Cates does not come to dinner. On Monday evening, when her father comes home from work, he asks her to come into the living room and sit on the sofa. He has something to tell her. The mohair upholstery scratches her thighs and makes her restless. As he leans toward her from his chair opposite and begins to speak, she thinks how different he sounds, saying each word separately as if he didn't think she would understand him.

"I have some very sad news, Claire. About our friend Fred Cates."

Not her friend. Not any more.

"He caught influenza and it got to be pneumonia. He died yesterday. I'm so sorry, Claire. He just died. It was a terrible shock to everybody." He stops for a minute, looks into her eyes and says, "Are you all right, honey?"

Of course she's all right. Fred Cates is dead. She won't see him again. All right. Fine. Now he is really erased. She waits until her father moves away from her. He goes off into the kitchen looking puzzled and sad. She gets up and goes into the sun room, picks up her rag doll, Ruthie, from the wicker chair where she had left her that morning. She hugs Ruthie to her chest and goes back into the hall. Her father's voice comes from the kitchen. He sounds angry.

"What's going on here? I thought she loved Fred. She looked at me like I said to get ready for school or something. No tears, nothing. What's the matter with her?"

Claire stops on the stairs, and holds her breath to hear her mother's answer.

"Probably just the shock. She'll cry later, I imagine. She's a private little thing. Want a drink before supper? I could use one."

That night, lying wide awake in her bed, ears straining to hear her parents talking in their room, their door open, assuming her to be asleep, she hears her mother say, "I can't take it in."

Tears in her voice. Her mother never cries.

"Put his shot gun in his mouth! My God, I had no idea things were that bad. I thought he'd make it. Get another job. Something."

And her father's voice answering, soothing, speaking to her mother in a way she has never heard him speak. It frightens her to hear it. 'Daddy sounds scared,' she thinks, and pulls the covers up, willing the sound of his voice away, hearing him anyway, through the blanket and the sheets.

"We'll make it, hon. We're okay. Poor devil. Too much for him."

Poor devil. Her father meant Fred Cates. Poor devil. So he must be in Hell. She hopes her mother won't have to go to Hell too for laughing at her. Maybe that was Fred Cates' fault.

'Daddy has a shotgun, too. It's big and scary,' Claire thinks and puts her left thumb, the one she sucked when she was little, into her mouth, closes her lips around it and begins to suck, slowly, rhythmically, with remembered ease. Her sucking brings saliva pouring into her mouth and she swallows thirstily. Finally, Ruthie hugged in the crook of her right elbow, she sleeps and has no dreams.

In time she will remember the Black Jack gum and the way Fred Cates smiled at her across the dinner table, looking into her eyes as if she were a real person. For now it's enough that he's gone.

1937

THE WELL

A Story

"We'll have to get the well in. Can't spend the summer here with no water," Tommy calls out to her without looking up from his work.

'Water's the least of it,' Mary thinks, standing in the open door of the cabin, looking out across the leveled earth to where her husband kneels beside two piles of rocks. He's been out since early morning sorting through them, lifting, studying, discarding.

'He's got a second pile as big as the first,' she thinks. 'All the stones that aren't fit for his wall.'

Mary knows the rhythm of his work. Even when she is in the cabin, cooking, cleaning, she sees him in her mind. He finds a rock that suits him, places it so it snugs into the narrow space between two of the stones already in place. He wedges a smaller stone into a crack, turning it this way and that until it slides into the crevice like a tenon into a mortise. She's seen him do that with wood. Slide the chiseled tongue into the snug slot, making a joint that will last forever. 'Dry wall', he calls what he's doing now with the rocks. No cement between the stones to hold them against frost heave. She loves to watch him handle the stones. The sure way his hands move is part of what keeps her with him. The anger she feels toward Tommy has not changed her love of the way he shapes something wonderful from whatever is at hand.

The log cabin where she stands in the door, watching him, has grown from his mind and hands. He bought the five mountain-top acres on which the cabin stands for next to nothing he had told her.

"Met a fella lost most of his acres to the bank. Damn fool needed a hundred dollars to save the rest of his farm."

Where the hundred dollars came from she doesn't know. They have nothing in the bank, nothing extra anywhere that she knows of. Tommy's kept his job at the aircraft factory in spite of the depression, the lay-offs everywhere. They always have rent money for the mock Tudor house on Elm Street in the small town outside of Hartford where they have lived for the ten years of their marriage. They have money for food and for a few new clothes over the years. Nothing to play with except what she squeezes from the grocery allowance.

Still, she hasn't questioned the hundred dollars or the cabin. This project of his seems to her an atonement or a wooing. Like the bird her father told her about when she was little. The bower bird's mating offering, she remembers, is an elaborate construction of grasses and twigs with a display of rocks or blossoms or found objects arranged on the ground in front of it. Not a nest but a plea. So far, she has refused to acknowledge that she sees an apology in Tommy's log cabin.

She has come with him every week-end through the fall and winter into the spring. She cooks on the huge cast iron wood stove that was the first piece of equipment hauled by pick-up truck up the mile and a half of rough track leading to the site.

For weeks she slept in a tent and now sleeps in a sleeping bag on the bare floor of the roughed-in cabin. This arrangement suits her. She needn't respond to Tommy's suggestions of intimacy. The sleeping bag provides privacy without the need for explanations.

During her waking hours she sees to what her mother calls her wifely duties. She keeps hot coffee available for Tommy and for the friends who come to help him. She cooks stews and soups and chili for all of them. Keeps nine-year-old Claire, their daughter, busy and out of the way. Or sends her to stay with her own mother, Claire's Grandma Fiske, for long week-ends. She does each thing pleasantly, without nagging, without question. And without forgiveness.

'That's what the cabin is,' she thinks, finally, 'More than any other thing, it's an apology.'

The cabin, thirty feet by twenty, of logs felled by him, trimmed by him, notched by him, hoisted into place by him with the help of one or two of their friends, shows her the size of his betrayal.

Now she thinks, 'What if there is no water up here at the top of a mountain? What if we have to pump it up from the river? It's going to cost a pretty penny no matter what. Not my worry, I guess.'

She smiles the half smile, lips together, that she wears when she speaks to Tommy these days, and calls out to him from the door, "Want lunch?"

He sits back on his heels, waiting, she thinks, for her to admire his handiwork. With a tiny thrill of pleasure she ignores him and his wall. She looks past him and calls to Claire. "Lunch, honey. Come on in and wash up."

Claire comes out of the trees at the top of the rise beyond the wall, runs down the slope toward the cabin, brushing her hands on her shorts, her thin shoulders and chest hidden under the large red cotton shirt she has adopted as her daily costume. Mary wore the shirt for years, then put it in the give-away box from which Claire has rescued it. For the first time she has defied Mary, has refused her request to wear something more suitable. Mary shrugs as she watches her tall, thin daughter walk down the hill toward her father.

'What does it matter out here in the woods. Let her do what she wants.'

Claire joins her father and they walk quickly toward the cabin, father in front, daughter just missing his heels as she follows.

'I'll give him lunch, but he won't get anything else from me,' Mary thinks, hugging her denial of him to her like the rag doll Claire still clutches to her chest at bed time.

She misses Tommy, misses their old ease and intimacy, but not enough to relent. She turns back into the large, open kitchen, with its walls of rough, unfinished split logs and its tar paper covered floor, thinking of her yellow and green kitchen at home with the gas stove and the electric refrigerator their landlord put in over a year ago. She glances at the oak ice box against the back wall. It is only slightly used, a gift from her mother, bartered from a neighbor for one of the beautiful afghans her mother crochets. The ice box has yet to hold a block of ice. No way for the ice man to get up the track. She keeps things cold outside in the winter and in a bucket of cold water from the river now that spring is here.

A roll of linoleum with its pattern of yellow diamonds on a light gray background leans against the ice box. It will be laid over the plywood and tar paper floor when everything else has been completed, when the walls are caulked, the roof shingled and the well dug. The linoleum is the only thing she has asked for since the cabin project began.

"I'd like a bright floor in the kitchen", she had said.

"The perfect thing," Tommy had answered. How clever of her to have thought of it. Overdoing it. Trying to win her back.

'What the hell, Tommy, it's only linoleum,' she had thought.

Still, she is pleased with her choice. Wants it to be laid last, after all the heavy traffic through the kitchen has eased.

Now she stands with her back to the sink, watching Tommy and Claire eat the sandwiches she's made for lunch.

Tommy handsome in his red and black flannel shirt, his cheeks flushed with energy. Claire sitting forward in her chair, her long fingers holding the triangle of bread carefully. Mary thinks, 'Like a guest in her own house'.

"I'll ask Jess Kusiak about his uncle. He's a dowser. Maybe he can find us some water. It's here all right. Just a question of finding it," Tommy says, brushing crumbs from his upper lip. Leaning both elbows on the makeshift plank table, he picks up his paper cup of milk and drains it in one swallow. Not looking at her. Talking into the air. Not sure he's having a conversation. Leaving information where she can find it if she's interested.

"What's a dowser, Daddy?" Claire asks, floating her question into this same space, not looking at her father, tending to her sandwich, her cup of chocolate milk.

He looks up, startled, Mary thinks, to find Claire there at the table with him.

"A dowser's a water witch, honey. A fellow who can find water with a forked willow twig."

Watching from where she stands by the sink, dish cloth forgotten in her hand, Mary sees Claire turn to her father, abandoning her sandwich, absorbed in his words. Mary has heard it all before. Tommy and her father, when he was alive, going on and on about the power of the dowser.

'Never seen it work. Not once,' she thinks.

She turns away from the two at the table and picks up the heavy aluminum tea kettle that she leaves simmering all day on the back of the stove. She carries it to the sink and pours a thin stream of steaming water into the dish pan and puts the kettle back on the stove. She swishes a few flakes of Ivory Soap around till a gray foam forms on the surface of the water, slides a crockery bowl, a mixing spoon and two blue and white china plates into the water. She wipes the dish cloth over the surface of the plates, inside the small bowl, puts them on the wooden drainboard to dry. She swishes her hands through the dish water, searching the murky bottom for the spoon, but her eyes are focused in the distance, on the stand of pine at the edge of the cleared space just outside the window above the sink. She doesn't hear the voices of her husband and daughter.

She is remembering all the winter weekends Boots and Ed Pollard have come to the cabin to help with the building. Remembering one New Year's Eve in particular. She had taken Claire over to stay with her Grandma Fiske for the week-end.

The four of them, Boots and Ed and Tommy and she, have snow-shoed up from the car to the cabin, carrying food and, in Ed's case, drink, for the long weekend. Ed supplements what he makes at the garage he owns with his brother by running a still in the woods behind his house. This weekend he has brought a half gallon of moonshine as his contribution to the celebration. Big, comfortable Ed and sharp little Boots. Older than Tommy and Mary. Mid-forties, maybe closer to fifty, Mary thinks.

"Never could figure them as a couple," Tommy always says. "What's she see in him?"

'And it's Ed who's his friend,' Mary thinks. Funny kind of loyalty. "What do *you* see in him?" she wants to ask, but the question would suggest a willingness on her part to discuss their friends in the old way, the way they used to talk together before, and so she doesn't ask.

Now, standing at the sink on a warm spring day, she is remembering the four of them, seated in front of the fire place on New Year's Eve, drinks of straight hootch in their hands, no light other than that from the four foot logs blazing in the huge stone fireplace, the fire light reaching only as far as the couch, leaving the rest of the huge, empty space as dark as a cave.

The ceiling, a story and a half above them, is a home for bats, Mary thinks. In the process of straightening up earlier in the day she has found the remains of a nest of mice under the cushions of the old couch that is the principle piece of furniture in the main room of the cabin. She has disposed of the tiny skeletons, the scraps of fur. Now it seems to her that the whole place is open to invasion by the wild life waiting just outside the door. Her safety lies within the reach of the firelight. She looks over at Ed, bearlike in his brown wool sweater, all but asleep on the couch. His feet resting on the cobbler's bench are huge in leather highcut boots, the raw hide laces untied and loosened. His round Slavic face ruddy with heat and alcohol, mouth curved in an absent smile, looks to Mary like the man-in-the-moon. She likes Ed and he likes her.

'We're easy with each other the way people who have no interest in climbing into bed together can be,' she thinks. 'Not flirtatious, like some I could name.'

Boots and Ed and Tommy have finished nearly half the jug of moonshine since noon. Mary has nursed three-quarters of a juice glass full of the nasty tasting liquor, loving the warmth that spreads through her chest and into her stomach, but not daring the loss of control that will follow if she has more.

There has been little work done on the sleeping loft they had planned to floor-in by this evening. They will sleep in front of the fire in their sleeping bags as they have nearly every weekend since the roof went on.

The only chairs they have brought to the cabin so far are the three mismatched kitchen chairs Jess Kusiak found in his father's barn and presented to Mary with a flourish, as if they had been a matched set of Windsor chairs.

Boots prefers to sit on the floor. She is small, four eleven, ninety pounds drawn tight and dry over her bones by alcohol and nicotine. She chain smokes Lucky Strikes, her claw fingers, nails blood red, tapping the next smoke from the package before the first is finished, lighting one from the other, grinding the stub out thoroughly, reluctantly. She doesn't speak till after the first deep pull on the new cigarette. As often as not, Mary has noticed, everyone around her will stop talking and watch Boots puff, tap, light, stub out, puff, before going back to their conversation. As if she had the power to addict everyone to her ritual.

Mary's mother has said more than once that Boots' skin is too dry for the rouge and powder she dusts on four or five times a day. "It just cakes up on her and rubs off on her clothes. Her collars never look fresh."

Mary hates to have her mother criticize Boots, but she is aware of the odor of *Evening in Paris*, stale and slightly rancid, that lingers in Boot's clothes. The smell is exotic, Mary thinks, part of Boots.

Boots' eyes are large and blue, the lashes heavy with Maybelline black mascara. Her hair on this particular New Year's Eve, is blond. Thin and short and permed. The color, Mary knows, comes from peroxide. Sometimes she helps Boots bleach her hair at the kitchen sink at home. Boots always teases her to bleach her own dark brown bob. She has been tempted, but has not succumbed, afraid of becoming someone she doesn't know.

Boots is tough and profane and like a honey pot to a bear cub where men are concerned. As if one of the boys had become a woman and was therefore available in a different way. Mary feels fat and awkward and plain around Boots. Hates her own plump cheeks and rounded body. Longs to be drawn thin and bright, like a tube of neon. Mary thinks of Boots as her best friend. Not that they exchange confidences. They play cards with two other neighborhood women occasionally. Mostly, they come together when their husbands are together. Mary doubts that she is Boots' best friend.

Tommy sits on an upended stump of log across from Boots. He sparkles in the shifting firelight, his auburn hair gleaming redder than it does in daylight, his brown eyes bright with reflected flame, his straight nose casting the right side of his face in partial shadow. To Mary, her blood warmed by the fire and by the careful sips of moonshine, he looks like a movie star, like a young Douglas Fairbanks. Her guard is down. If he asked her to forgive him at this moment she would say, "For what?" She leans her head against the couch, lulled and sleepy, and gazes at her husband. It takes her a long moment to realize that he is looking straight at Boots. Talking straight to Boots. Focusing his energy on Boots.

"You sure do make a party, Bootsie. Wouldn't have been much fun without you. You know how to make a fella feel good."

Mary, her heart stopped, her body suddenly upright on the couch, thinks, 'As if we're not here, Ed and me, for cripe's sake. Right back to his old tricks.'

For nearly a year she has been sure of Tommy's betrayal and has left the discovery unexplored. She has not known who her enemy might be and has not until tonight thought it might be Boots. She looks over at Ed. He is smiling broadly now. Drunk and happy and nearly asleep.

'If he were awake he wouldn't care,' she thinks. 'He likes it that Tommy thinks she's cute.'

Boots looks into Tommy's eyes and says, "Get out of here. Ed may be an old fart but he's my old fart and I'm not looking to change my luck with the likes of you." She grins when she says it and Tommy grins back.

Boots can say anything to a man and make him like it, Mary thinks.

Tommy reaches across the open face of the fire place and puts his hand on Boots' knee. Mary watches his fingers slide along Boots' thigh, close on the fabric of her slacks, squeeze the flesh with the tips of his fingers. Boots does not look at Tommy. She finishes her drink and shifts her position on the floor so that Tommy's hand slides from her leg.

Mary feels the heat from the fire using up all the air in the room. She gets up from the couch too quickly, stumbles as she walks back into the kitchen, her throat tight and her hands shaking.

In the shadowed dark she feels for the oil lamp on the counter, finds the box of Ohio kitchen matches next to the lamp and strikes a match against the box. She blinks at the sudden flare of light, lifts the glass chimney and holds the match to the lamp wick. The petal of flame blooms in the dark and with her left hand she settles the chimney back into the metal clips that hold it firm. The match is in her right hand, burning close to her fingers. She blows it out and stands looking at the reflection of the lamp light on the black surface of the window over the sink.

She says aloud, "I'd be better off out there in the dark. I'm suffocating in here."

She goes over to the wood stove, takes the lid lifter from the warming shelf above the stove, inserts it into the slot in the round iron cover of the big back burner, lifts the cover and places it to one side. She reaches down to the pile of short logs in the crate beside the stove and picks up a two foot piece of pine. She puts it in the stove and reaches for another log. When the wood has caught, she replaces the lid and calls out to the others, "Coffee, anybody? I'm going to have some before I turn in. Anybody else?"

No one answers.

'Go to hell,' she thinks.

The sudden sound of Claire's voice startles her back to the sight of Claire and Tommy still at the table, talking. She has time to think, 'I didn't give in to him. I didn't shame myself. Thank God,' before she turns to her daughter.

"Mommy, Daddy says I can try dowsing when the man comes to find our well," Claire says.

Before she answers Mary walks past the table to the stove, pot holder in hand, picks up the tea kettle and carries it to the sink where she tips the steaming water carefully, miserly, over the dishes stacked there, rinsing them of soap. She has no desire to spoil her daughter's joy, but she can't share it, stemming as it does from Tommy.

'I've become a bitch,' she thinks. The word is hard for her. 'He's been a bastard and I've become a bitch.'

"We'll have to see, Claire, when Jess' uncle gets here."
Her answer is cold and mean, she thinks, as she watches Claire's face go from open to guarded. 'It's the best I can do. She's used to me. She won't die of it.'

Mary hears the truck laboring up the last quarter mile of rough track to the cabin. It's a rare sound. She and Tommy usually park the Pontiac in a cleared pull-off at the base of the mountain and carry their gear up to the cabin. Sometimes it takes two long, hard-breathing trips to get everything from the car. She is torn between wanting the road scraped and leveled and wanting to keep the privacy that the all but impassable track has given them for the past nine months.

The truck belongs to Jess Kusiak. He's bringing his uncle up to try for water. Tommy has met his uncle briefly at Jess' house, but he is a stranger to Mary. She is shy of strangers and has spent the past half hour readying herself and the cabin for this unknown man's arrival. She would not have bothered for Jess. Jess works at the plant with Tommy. He's not a favorite of hers in spite of his help with the cabin. He is small and dark and reminds Mary of a drawing of John Wilkes Booth in a book of her father's. Jess is not married and he plays fast and loose with the women, according to Boots. He is always perfectly polite to Mary. Too polite, she thinks. Not easy, like Ed. On his best behavior. Her mother has never trusted men who are too polite, too careful of their language and Mary knows her mother doesn't like Jess. She doesn't like Tommy much, come to that.

"Can't keep his eyes at home. You're too good for him, Mary."

Maybe so.

"'Morning, Mary. Beautiful day," Jess calls to her as he drops down out of the cab of the truck

He is wearing work clothes, black flannel shirt and khaki pants, his black hair pomaded, wet looking, like a stone from the bottom of the river.

"Tommy's done a lot since last week. Just look at that wall. Sure has a way with stone, that husband 'a yours. Where is the great man? I've got Uncle Janos in the truck."

Jess waves his hand in the direction of the truck. Mary sees a man sitting in the passenger seat but can't make out his features. He appears tall and thin. His left hand, resting lightly on his knee, is lit by sunlight through the open driver's side door. Mary catches her breath as her eyes rest on the long, thin fingers, the dark hairs along the back of the quiet hand. He makes no move to leave the truck

Mary thinks, 'He wants me to go back in the cabin. Dowsing is man's work.' It's as if he has spoken to her, asked her to leave. She realizes he has not so much as turned his head in her direction. Certainly he has not spoken.

'Water witch,' she thinks with a shiver.

"I'll go find Tommy. He's out back. He's decided we need a porch overlooking the river. I'll get him," she calls up to Jess. 'I'm talking too much. Don't need to explain anything to Jess,' she thinks. "Something odd about that Janos," she says aloud, the sunlit image of his hand clearer in front of her than the ground she is walking over.

She goes into the cabin and walks back to the newly cut door leading out onto a platform that runs the length of the house. There is no railing yet and it makes Mary giddy to stand out here, perched over the steep, wooded ravine that ends at the river three hundred feet below. She sees Tommy, squatting at the far end of the porch, nails in his mouth, hammering at a framework of boards spread out on the rough platform. 'The railing,' she thinks with relief. The porch will be nice when she can feel safe on it, but she won't say so.

"Jess is here with the dowser," is what she says.

Tommy spits the nails into his hand, lays them aside with the hammer. He stands and walks toward her, smiling. He will not admit to her reserve, to what she thinks of as her cold shoulder. He is cheerful. Happy in his work. 'So damned sure he'll win me over,' she thinks angrily.

"I'll get coffee," she says over her shoulder as they walk through the house to the front. He will find nothing to criticize in her behavior.

"Good, hon. Thanks," he says on his way out to greet the men.

A quarter of an hour later Mary steps from the back door, a tray of steaming tin cups in her hands. There is no one in sight. She places the tray on Tommy's stone wall and walks to the side of the cabin. Deep in the woods, at the edge of a small glade, the red of Claire's shirt shows her where to look. Jess and Tommy and Claire stand in filtered sunlight, in a semi-circle, watching Uncle Janos cut a low branch from a tree.

'Like statues,' she thinks. She smiles and finds that she can't look away from the tableau, from the face of Janos. She feels she's looking at him through binoculars, his features perfectly clear, even at this distance. Hair as black as Jess' but full and thick. No Vitalis. He is in profile, his high forehead and jutting chin balanced by his beak of a nose. She imagines the deep, dark eyes set in the shadow of his heavy brow. His hands, one holding a shiny woodsman's knife, the other grasping the twig, are graceful. Mary wants to kiss them, to feel them on her body. She is warm, now, and moist, as she has not been for Tommy for longer than she can remember. A year at least. She is rapt. She imagines Janos' hands moving over her breasts, her hips, sure and possessive. Mary moves backward to the wall and sits without taking her eyes from the scene before her.

"Mommy, come see. Uncle Janos has the twig we need. We're going to find water."

Claire's voice seems to come from a great distance. She has to speak again, insist that her mother come see the wonder of Uncle Janos.

"Come over here, Mommy. Please come."

Mary focuses her eyes with difficulty, sees her daughter standing in front of her.

"Come on, little one. You shall help me. Children are good dowsers."

Janos is calling to Claire. Mary, hearing his voice for the first time, is surprised. There is something foreign in it, something she can't remember having heard in any other voice. A kind of formality that pleases and unsettles her. She stands and turns to face the three men, gathered now at the top of the rise in front of the house. She tests the earth with the toes of her sneakers before taking a step toward them.

"Uncle Janos, this is Mary, Tommy's wife, lucky dog," Jess says, holding his hand out to her as if to help her up the last of the rise.

Mary ignores him and walks over to stand beside Tommy, needing to be near him suddenly, the way Claire comes to her when there are strangers. But Claire hasn't come to her with Janos' arrival. She stands next to him, looking up into his face, eager and open. A different Claire. Mary nods in Janos' direction, not meeting his eyes.

"Happy to meet you, missus. You got a fine girl here," he says. He hasn't moved, but Mary feels as if he has bowed to her.

"I've brought coffee," she says and moves away again, back toward the house, feeling his eyes on her back.

Mary goes into the cabin. The kitchen is warm with the heat of the stove. She never lets the stove go out completely. Keeps it banked and the tea kettle on to moisten the air. Now she finds the heat too much. She needs shade, fresh air. She walks through the house onto the front deck and sits on the bare boards with her back against the stone of the chimney. She breathes in the smell of pine. A half hour has passed before she is calm.

'What's the matter with me? Close as I've ever come to the vapors.'

Her mother calls any kind of emotional excess the vapors. It is the first time Mary has used the words. It is the first time she has understood their meaning. Janos gives her the vapors. She will stay out of his way.

Mary has spent the day indoors. No one has missed her. In late afternoon, as she peels potatoes for supper, she hears Claire calling, "Mommy, I found it. I found water! Mommy, come see."

Mary puts the pot of peeled, quartered potatoes on the stove, fills the pot with water from the pail on the floor by the sink, and goes to the back door, drying her hands on a dish towel as she goes. She steps out onto the dirt of what Tommy calls the front yard and looks around for Claire.

Tommy, Jess and Janos are gathered around Claire in a space at the side of the cabin forty feet or so from the cabin wall. Claire holds the arms of a dowsing wand lightly in her small hands, the long stem of the 'y' formed by the branch pointing down toward the earth. Claire is absolutely still, her eyes on the willow twig, her expression contained and proud. The men around her are smiling, laughing with one another. Tommy has his hand on his daughter's shoulder.

'When was the last time he touched Claire?' Mary wonders. She glances at Janos and finds him looking at her. She turns her head to look back at her transfigured daughter.

"She did it," Janos says with a smile, "The young miss did it. You'll have water here."

"Good for you, Claire. Good for you," she says and begins to walk toward her daughter, deciding to dare the space near Janos for Claire's sake. The words she has said to Claire have come naturally. 'She's a good kid. Deserves better than she gets from me,' she thinks.

"She just walked over here straight as an arrow and the wand dipped down. Never saw a thing like it," Jess says. "I'll get my cousin to come up and dig the well. He needs some work on his house. Said he'd swap for some man hours. Okay with you, Tombo?"

"Sure, Jess. Great. That'll save me a bundle. Let me know when he can start. I'll be freed up here in a week or so. I can finish this place in August, once we get water."

Mary watches Tommy walk off toward the truck with Jess and Janos. They have forgotten her. Forgotten Claire. She sees them huddle at the truck, punching each other's arms in mutual congratulation at finding water. Jess and Tommy, that is. She notices that neither of them touches Janos. He smiles with them, but he is not one of them.

'Of course not,' Mary thinks. 'He's from another place.'

"Time for dinner," she says to Claire. "You've had a very exciting day, sweetie. I made chocolate pudding for dessert. We'll celebrate having our very own dowser."

Claire runs ahead of her into the house. Tommy follows them into the kitchen. They have a quiet supper and go to sleep early in front of the fire, each in his own sleeping bag.

For Mary, the return to the house on Elm Street has the comfort of the familiar. She spends the next week cleaning her kitchen, washing her curtains, putting aside on the guest room bed the clothes they will need for the summer. Getting the suitcases from the attic. She will pack on Friday for their return to the cabin on Saturday.

Tommy has been going back and forth to the cabin every night after work.

Mary's mother says, "If that's where he is. If that's what he's doing. You never know."

Mary ignores her mother's barbs. She knows Jess' cousin Harry has set up his well digger and has been working ten and twelve hour days since Monday. She knows, too, that Tommy can't stay away from machinery, that the fascination of the well-digger will keep him at the cabin.

"Had to blast," Tommy told her on Wednesday. "Bound to be rock that high up."

He hasn't said much since then and she hasn't asked for more. If the water is in they will stay at the cabin, she and

Claire, from now until September, when Claire will have to come back for school. For now, Tommy will drive the long drive in to work each week day morning and drive the long drive back to them each night.

'It will be hard for him, but it's his choice,' Mary thinks.

As much as she loves her home, as much as she thinks of the cabin as Tommy's place, she looks forward to the quiet of the mountain top. To the clear, warm days and cool nights, and the quiet. Claire is no trouble. She loves the woods, the river, the freedom.

'That's what I love too, The freedom,' Mary thinks, 'from the damn pot luck rent parties every weekend. From beggars at the door. They'll never find us way up there in the woods. From the scrimping. Don't need much at the cabin. We can make do with very little. If he doesn't start inviting the world to stay with us. And if he doesn't—' She leaves the thought unfinished.

The tangible proof that he has found some woman more desireable than he finds her, frightens her so that she can't entertain it. She has labeled it his 'sin' and has avoided dealing with it. She has only now and then allowed her anger to flare, the way it did on New Year's Eve. She has kept her silence for all of the months since the day more than a year ago when she found the crumpled handkerchief that was not hers in the back seat of the Pontiac.

She had placed the small, wrinkled bit of lace on his pillow that night. He had picked it up with his thumb and forefinger and dropped it in the wastebasket beside the bureau. He had said nothing. The next week he had started plans for the cabin.

On Saturday morning they pack the car and drive in silence the long, familiar miles to the all but invisible turn off on the wooded, mountain road. Claire, sitting on her suitcase in the back seat, falls asleep a few minutes after they start. Mary puts her head back and closes her eyes.

Tommy is a good driver and she is tired, ready to give herself over to the sound of the tires on the pavement. She sits up as she feels the car slow for the turn, but Tommy does not swing the wheel sharp right into their usual parking place. He guns the motor and starts up the track.

"Tommy, what are you doing?" she gasps, afraid for the Pontiac, afraid for herself and Claire on the steep, rocky track.

Tommy doesn't answer and she realizes that the track has been leveled. Rocks have been removed, rolled away over the edge of the rise. It is a road. Not paved, not smooth, but a road.

'Surprise, surprise,' she thinks, happy but unwilling to concede her pleasure.

They drive on and up, the car complaining only slightly, until they come to the last hill, the approach to the cabin. Tommy pulls the car into a cleared space under a pine and turns off the motor. He turns to Mary and smiles.

"What do you think of that, hon? Some road, huh? Harry came up with a bull dozer last week and did it. I owe him another week of work on his house, but it's worth it."

Mary smiles, not at him, but a smile. An acknowledgement of the job done, of the comfort and convenience provided.

'The ice man can come up now,' she thinks and her smile widens.

Claire is in the cabin by the time they have lifted the suitcases out onto the pine needle covered ground. Mary hears her call from the kitchen, "It's here. It's here. I can pump the water!"

Mary sees that the well digger is gone. The mountain top is theirs again, the silence and the birds and the rush of the river all those yards below. She walks to the cabin carrying a bag of groceries and stands in the doorway looking into the kitchen. Her linoleum is in place. Her kitchen looks bright and warm and finished. Her daughter stands at the sink, at the new pump, raising the long pump handle up and pushing it down as if she has always drawn water in this way. On the up stroke there is a thick sucking sound and on the down stroke water splashes into the sink.

Claire is letting the clear stream run over her hands, her arms. She catches water in a tin cup and releases the pump handle to drink.

"It's good, Mommy. It's cold and good. Uncle Janos said it would be the coldest water I'd ever drink."

"And the purest, honey," Tommy says, coming up behind Mary and putting the suitcases down, carefully, on the kitchen floor.

'On my new linoleum,' Mary thinks.

Claire holds out a tin cup filled to spilling with water from the well. Mary takes the cup and sips from it, the icy liquid numbing her teeth, her throat. She turns to Tommy, who is standing quietly behind her, waiting like a child to be noticed, she thinks. She lifts the cup to his lips. He sips from it, his eyes bright with tears.

"Janos was right," Mary says, "It's the coldest water I've ever tasted."

ISLAND WATER

at last
the blue-white glacier backs off
one centimeter at a time
leaving this shelf of sand
in the slowly warming ocean

so that now
on a day in summer
the water from our well runs cold
and tastes of polar ice

DAYTRIPPERS

a flight of pastel packable rainwear birds
migrating from Boston to Miami via Hyannis
has landed on Nantucket
muddling in the middle of a crosswalk
scratching at cobblestones
and clucking
    which way
    which way
a grey-polled yellow female
raises a sudden wing
and pointing to the right
squawks
    this way
    this way
the flock forms up and Vees off down the street

willy-nilly they have found a leader
and are headed South

BLACK-CROWNED NIGHT HERON

Saturday Morning on Hither Creek

yarmulka set firmly on the top of his head
shiny black coat settled on hunched shoulders
white prayer shawl down his chest on either side

he stands ankle deep in reeds
contemplating the empty pond
no congregation gathered for morning prayers

three mallards swim up to him, late for service
not enough to form a minyan
he dismisses them and davens by himself

walking in the sabbath dawn
we spot this rabbi at his avian devotions
we have never seen so reverent a bird

AUGER MOON

auger moon bored a hole through my dream
people do go mad when such things happen
bright night sifted through the hole
and woke me to madness
and to magic
the known world turned to silver
and I awake to see it
no wonder people call us lunatics
who live our dreams

VACATION

we travel toward the smell of brine on numbered routes
familiar signals ride the surface swell of expectation
       bobbing like buoys
Rehoboth   Deep River   To the Cape and Islands

in the deeper undertow free floating angst
       if you die first what will become of me
       what if Yugoslavia disintegrates
       babies in Ireland suckle on the death we send as gifts
       in our towns bare homeless flesh beds down on concrete
       if I die first what then of you

at bedrock where tides are barely felt
       and the world lives without sun
primal themes rock gently in the quiet dark

       has been   is   will be
       is   has been   will be
       will be   is   has been

a sea gull screams
the sign says *To the Dock*
we board the ferry and the ocean takes us to the island

ashore we say goodby to numbered routes
walk the known moors and climb remembered dunes
and live as if this life were all

WEEKEND ON NANTUCKET

i

ferried on the flood
the pair of us
watch for the dove
it is a gull, finally
that calls us to the rail
"We are saved !"
we shout
at the sight of Ararat's gray houses

ii

a single swan arrows across the sky
pulling the breath from our mouths
alone, I say, surprised
I know they mate for life
we turn to see the swan again
in each other's eyes

iii

over dunes to the sea
we find veiled sun
wide reach of sand
and yellow-green transluscence
    where the horizon will be on another day
today fog lies at the rim of the world
and where it touches land
turns to smoke
we think the sand is burning

SEA CHANGE

the summer house is life on a different plane
old rules do not apply
long days of idleness are not suspect
an hour's walk along the sand
or the digging of clams for half a day
are looked upon as industry
to be applauded or distained
according to one's view of life
as seen from the beach chair
we give each other galaxies of space
and watch no clocks
we eat when we are hungry
and sleep when we must
in touch with our circadian selves
our talk is gentle discourse
no louder than the shore birds
nor as filled with news
we city ants
become grasshoppers for a time
in the joy of simple pleasure
we are improvident

MADAKET ROAD

twelve o six a m on the Madaket Road
three yearlings
single file and washed with fog

you glide the Volvo to a stop

silenced by the presence of the deer
and by three glasses each of Pouilly Fume with dinner
we sit in stop time
watching the deer pass a sobriety test
down the double yellow line

one certain little hoof after the other

JULY AFTER MILLIE

the fog has gone
and left the daisies
the Madaket sky is swept of all but blue
towels on clotheslines
snap and crack in sea wind
like the sails of the Rainbow Fleet
the harbor chops enough to give her ducks a bumpy ride
Millie's is all new shingles
windows let into the sides
admit the light she never sought
nor missed

whoever rents the place
will have a ghost to deal with
and should be warned

SUMMER HOUSE IN WINTER

wakened by separate dreams
we stand on cold kitchen tile
to stare at black windows
and wait a silent dawn

the sun rising late and in the wrong place
backlights distant pines
and deepens shadows
then inches high enough to wash the whole scene flat
    with morning light

that too short day we give each other space
sharing only the unexpected chill
of rooms where we have known the summer

we watch the sun set
this time too early and too far to the left
it drops without preamble
and without a hint of color

at the dark edge of the world
we are left watching the dipper form too low
we wonder how to get our bearings
in this familiar place
    in this unfamiliar time

MEMOIR

There is the feeling of rough beard, of whisker burn. I have been lifted up to sit on the hospital bed where my grandfather lies dying. Whoever lifted me says "Kiss your grandfather, Shirley" so I do and my cheek is rasped by his beard. Days later he is dead and for many years I know nothing more of him than that he hurt me. My mother, the second of four children of Elbert and Florence and the first of two girls, tells me what I now know of him. She tells me over time as people do in a family. A few words here and there.

"We played cards on Sunday but only when my father went for his constitutional, his Sunday walk. He was a preacher, you know. Kind of strict, but I loved him."

"He was a very quiet man. I don't think he and my mother were suited. She had more imagination."

"They were divorced. It was a good thing, but it came too late. Hard for both of them. Hardly anyone divorced in those days."

And then the final thing.

"I used to watch my mother, your grandmother, hang the laundry on the clothesline in our backyard in Indiana. She'd take a sheet, shake it out and peg the hem to the line. Then she'd take another sheet but she wouldn't shake it out. She'd just peg it to the first one and then fold the bottom of the first one up and peg it. The second sheet was inside the first, hidden. One day I snuck up when she went back in the house and pulled the sheets apart. The one on the inside had holes in it. Round holes that were hemmed and even, meant to be there, eyeholes, and I knew in that minute that my father was a member of the Ku Klux Klan. Once I was downtown in Indianapolis with my boyfriend and there was a parade and there was my father right at the head of it with his Klan hood pulled back so you could see his face. I was too embarrassed to speak. I never told him I saw him. We never talked about it."

She said that he adored me. Carried me around with him to all his favorite haunts, the cigar store, the drug store, the billiard parlor, where he showed me off. At two, I spoke well and clearly and he loved that. I'm sure it's all true, but my cheek remembers the sharp sting of his dying beard and it's hard to believe he didn't mean to hurt me.

* * *

Teddy gave me two rabbits for my fifth birthday. Peter, the handy man, a large dark person whom I adored, built hutches for them in back of the house on Main Street in Windsor, Connecticut. Teddy lived next door. He was a year older than I and I loved him, too. I fell in love with everyone when I was young. This one is tall and thin and has bright red finger nails. This one is tiny and round and smells of ginger. This one has a blind eye and a big laugh and can lift me to the sky. Love at first sight or scent or touch. I had crushes on my school mates, boy friends in every grade and it didn't matter if my affections were returned. Being the one who loved was what mattered. And Teddy deserved my heart. He shared his spearmint Christmas tree shaped lollipop with me. I can taste it now. He walked me to school every morning, the long blocks to Stony Hill School, the one room school house where I was in kindergarten and he was in first grade. Our teacher, Mrs. Kelso, taught whatever we were ready to learn without regard to grade assignment. I sat next to Teddy and shared his Primer and fell in love with reading. And he gave me two rabbits for my birthday. I feel now the soft fur of the brown rabbit against the skin of my arms as I held it on that fifth day of September in 1932, the surprising sharpness of its claws digging into my flesh so that I dropped it to the ground. Teddy and I chased it under the hedge that stood between our houses until we caught it between us and carried it back, quivering, to its mate in the hutch. The next year we moved again and I walked to school alone.

* * *

The time we spent at air fields, my mother and I, waiting for my father to take off or land or to finish checking the engine of his plane is all one in my memory. My mother says it was every Sunday until I was almost three. After my brother was born in June of 1930, we spent less time in hangars and on the aprons of hangars and on the grass verges of air fields and more time waiting for my father at home, together, the three of us.

What I remember of those early Sundays is the smell of grease and gasoline which I loved and still love. And the shapes of the airplanes, one with the wing set low on the fuselage, one with two wings and a huge dark engine. And hearing my father yell 'contact' from his open seat, watching his mechanic, the man he called his grease monkey, spinning the propeller until the engine coughed and caught and roared, pulling the chocks from under the wheels of the plane and my father moving away, going faster and faster until he was in the air, flying over our heads, dipping the wings of the plane to say 'goodbye, see you later'. I remember playing in the hangar, the metal ceiling so high above my head it was in shadow, the cement floor, oil spotted and rough under my feet, the tool boxes and storage spaces, not frightening but mysterious. I ran between the planes, under the wings, touching the wheels of the planes, the tires fat and hard as stone to my small fingers. This place belonged to my father and he would be back before the afternoon was over, his plane hanging low in the sky, coming fast toward my mother and me where we stood on the concrete apron of the hangar, the tires squealing once as they touched the tarmac, the propeller slowing and then stopping, and my father standing up in the cockpit, climbing down to the metal step on the wing, his good leg first (the one I called his real leg, the other having been amputated in a farm accident when he was ix and replaced with a heavy wood and leather strap-on leg), then onto the solid ground holding his arms out to me. I remember how he smelled and how he looked, but I've lost his voice except for the resonance. He was glad to see me. I was safe and I was powerful.

* * *

The syringes my father used to inject himself with adrenaline when his asthma was bad were so beautiful that I felt deprived that I could not have one. Could not touch one. I don't think now that I was supposed to know they existed. But I did. I saw them in the pan on the stove when my mother boiled them to be sure they were sterile. I saw them on the bedside table on the mornings after my father had had a really bad night trying to breath, his lungs unresponsive and inelastic with years of asthma. I saw them when I peeked through the bedroom door to watch him hold up the bottle of medicine, pierce the membrane at the neck of it with the long, silver needle that was the nose of the syringe, push the air out of the needle with a tiny spray of liquid, slide the needle into the pinched up flesh of his thigh, and push the plunger that emptied the syringe into his leg. I wanted to do that. I wanted to help him by doing all those wonderful things with that beautiful shiny syringe. The sleek glass tube, marked to show the centimeters, the plunger that slid so effortlessly to suck in and then to release the medicine, and that perfect needle with a hole through the middle of it (how tiny that hole must be) to deliver the medicine under my father's blue and desiccated and scary looking skin so that he could take another breath without wheezing, coughing, choking. The syringe made my father feel better and I wanted one.

* * *

I remember the taste of Campbell's Cream of Tomato Soup, tart and sweet at the same time, and the smell of the white bread toast my mother made to go with the soup when I came home from school at lunch time, quivering with hunger. The toast was crisp at the edges and soft with melted butter in the middle and I would eat a whole piece of toast first before I could slow down enough to spoon the soup away from me and swallow it without slurping.

When my mother left my father and took my brother with her to Michigan I stayed on in our apartment on Main Street in East Hartford with my mother's mother, Grandma Rough. I was nine and I was told I couldn't miss school. I had to stay put while my brother went off to Niles to be with my mother and my aunt and my cousins. My grandmother gave me tomato soup and toast for lunch each day. It didn't satisfy. It was just toast and soup and nothing else.

Grandma's youngest child, my Uncle Rink was with us then, Grandma Rough and me. I remember riding in his old Ford or maybe it was my father's car or maybe he borrowed a car from someone. I remember it as his old Ford. He'd come into my bedroom, the room I shared with my brother who wasn't there in the other twin bed any more. He'd pick me up in a blanket and carry me to the car and we'd chase fire engines. If it turned out to be a big fire we'd go to a drug store to get a pint of coffee ice cream for each of us and a package of Walnettos. We'd sit and eat watching the firemen stream water on the blaze from the safety of the car. I remember hiding in my mother's clothes closet and writing on the wall with a red crayon *I hate Rink*. He couldn't bring my mother back and he couldn't do anything about the *dirty blond in Dayton* my father's men friends teased about. So for all Rink's kindness, because he wasn't able to make things right, I wrote those words. I sat in the dark on the floor with my mother's shoes around me, the few pair she had left here in her home, the smell of her on the dresses hanging above me, and I cried as I marked the closet wall with my red crayon, scared at the magnitude of what I was doing. As far as I know, Rink never saw what I had written. He never mentioned it if he did, but then he wouldn't have.

My grandmother let my father visit only once during the six weeks of my mother's absence. Or maybe he came only once. I sat on the living room couch with him as if he were a stranger. It was his own couch in his own living room and he sat there like a visitor. It was the most uncomfortable I'd ever been in the company of an adult and I was with my own father. I remember not knowing what to say. I didn't say "Why are you making my Mommy sad?" I didn't ask when he would be coming home, if he would be coming home. I don't remember if he talked at all. He gave me a stuffed Mickey Mouse wearing a Stetson and chaps and two guns in holsters. My father loved cowboys and the hat he wore that I liked best was a Stetson. I still have Mickey. He's lost his guns and his hat and I had to sew on new eyes long ago. Mickey was an apology, I thought so when I was nine and I think so now.

※　※　※

I remember Mrs.Peck blowing on her pitch pipe. We were having music instead of arithmetic so I knew it was Friday. Monday was art and Friday was music. I was in the fourth grade in another new school and it was hard to concentrate on things like the times-tables. All I could think about was that my mother and brother were living in Michigan and my father was miles away in Glastonbury with his mother while I was living in our apartment with my grandmother. I remember trying to do all the things that were expected of me, to keep the usual order in my life, but I hadn't been able to swallow my breakfast that morning around the lump in my throat.

The sound of that one note on the pitch pipe made me happy for a moment. Singing, not arithmetic. I sang the first words of the song with the rest of the class. "'Mid pleasures and palaces, though we may roam" but when I had to start the next line "Be it ever so humble, there's no place like home", tears burst from my eyes and poured down my cheeks. I sobbed out loud and was too unhappy to be embarrassed. I wanted to be at home, whatever that meant. Mother or no mother. Alone or with my grandmother, I didn't care. Just let me be home. The word was bigger than any place or person. It filled me so full there wasn't room for anything else. I remember lifting my head up from my desk, tears running down my face and into the collar of my blouse, and seeing Mrs. Peck walk down the aisle toward me, her short body in a dark dress, passing easily between the desks. I remember thinking she must be angry with me for disturbing the class, but she wasn't. She put her arm over my shoulders and said something about my not feeling well and that she was going to send me home. I remember rushing from my seat, not saying anything to Mrs. Peck, running the long blocks home, sobbing with relief. I remember thinking I could stand going to school now because, if I couldn't bear it, Mrs. Peck would let me go home.

* * *

The little people were bigger than fairies. They were almost up to my knees though I never got close enough to measure. I was four and we were living in a big house with a beautiful long stairway in the front hall. It was made of a dark wood that was so shiny I could see it glowing even when the hall lights were out. Mary was a teenager who took care of me sometimes and she called the stairway a mountain. She and I would climb the mountain side, picking flowers as we went. Wild flowers. Mary knew the names of all of them but buttercup is the only one I remember. By the time we reached the top step our make believe basket would be filled with make believe blossoms and Mary would walk with me into my bedroom and put me to bed. I learned long afterwards that Mary and Ruth and the others who stayed with us through those years were the daughters of families who were having a hard time finding enough to eat, enough to wear, enough coal to stay warm, in the years of the Great Depression. They and thousands of others like them, were taken in or hired by the week by slightly more fortunate families. The girls helped with the children and with the cleaning and in return they were fed and clothed and given a little money which most of them shared with their families. What I knew then was that Mary was my friend. She knew stories and games and she never said something wasn't if I said it was, but I don't remember if I ever told her about the little people. I told my grandmother. She never said she saw them but she never said I didn't. The little people were filmy, like cigarette smoke. They moved that way, too. Swaying and drifting through the hall at the bottom of the stairs, their wispy feet not touching the floor. They were a blue-gray color and they made a humming sound as they moved. I saw them often, but I never thought they were interested in me. They would float near me for a moment and then slide off into the shadows. The only thing they ever told me was that they were cold. I don't remember hearing the words. I just knew. And that's what I told my grandmother. The little people have no warm clothes. They're cold. I sat with her and we went through her scrap bag finding little bits of velvet or printed cotton she said she could use to make something warm. I see her now sitting in a chair under the standing lamp, stitching the bright scraps into skirts and shirts and jackets. We put them all into a shoe box and left it on the bottom stair. In the morning the box and all the tiny clothes were gone. I wasn't surprised. Mary wouldn't have been surprised, either, if I'd told her.

* * *

Ginny Roberts lived next door when we were on Maple Street in Windsor. I had my sixth birthday in that house and Ginny came to my party. A boy from the next street over came, too. Paul. Small with light hair and a nice smile. He and I had become quick and fast friends on sight. I don't remember Ginny going with me to his house to play. Paul and I played in his garage where there was a cot and a box of his father's tools and not much else. Mostly we wrestled and chased each other around in the semi-dark. I remember having supper with his family one night. He had several siblings but I don't know now if they were brothers or sisters or how many there were. Just that dinner at their table was noisy and the food was scarce. I had bread and butter, that much I'm sure of, but if there was anything else it has left my memory. One afternoon after school he and I were battling some imagined enemy in the garage when, to my horror, I put my foot through one of the cobwebbed windows. I kicked as high and as hard as I could and heard glass shattering before I felt my foot push through the pane and out into the afternoon air. I wasn't hurt but I was frightened and ashamed. I don't remember anyone yelling at me or punishing me, but I did realize that from the little they had I had taken something tangible.

A few months later, Paul died. His mother had given him an enema and had punctured his bowel. My mother told me that, I don't know why. It was the first death that I remember. When my grandfather died, they must have told me about it, but I have no memory of a funeral or of missing him. This was different. Whenever I walked by his house, past his garage, I felt sad and uneasy, as if I were missing something in the explanation of my friend's death. I had nightmare pictures in my mind of what his mother had done to him, but where was he? How could his family sit down to dinner without him? My mother talked with me. She wanted me to know that his mother was broken hearted, that she hadn't meant to hurt him. But she couldn't keep him safe and what did that mean to me? The sense of his having had so little, so few toys, none that I remember, and so short a life stayed with me. Most of our friends, my parents' and mine, had less than enough, but playing in that garage, eating at that table with Paul was the first time that I knew what it was to be truly poor. I wondered what I would have to do to stay safe, how good I would have to be to keep from being poor and hungry or dead.

But we always had enough to share with those who were temporarily out of something, flour or potatoes or bread, and over time I felt secure again. Ginny and I played house and store and school. Her grandmother, a very old woman, much older than my Grandma Rough, crocheted tiny rugs for the doll house my father had made for my fifth Christmas and Ginny and I made clothes-pin people to live in the house. I remember how good I felt putting the wooden family in their beds and covering them with handkerchiefs, making them safe for the night.

* * *

My mother's clothes, her jewelry, her pocket books were the essence of her. They were what it meant to be a grown woman. I watched her put on her plain white cotton underwear, her white rayon slip, her washed and ironed house dress or, if there was to be a party, her one evening gown, blue velvet with a narrow taffeta ruffle at the scoop neck and at the hem or her 'good dress', the details of which I don't remember. I memorized all of her motions. She would be in her underpants and she would bend forward to let her breasts fall into the cups of her bra, then stand and fasten the hooks and eyes behind her back. I would go around behind her to watch her fingers work. How does she do that? How can she tell where the loops are? She would slide her arms into the slip which lay on her bed, raise her arms above her head and let the slip drop down her body until her hands and then her arms emerged from the arm holes and she would adjust the straps on her shoulders. Sometimes she would move her hands down over her hips and the smooth sound of the rayon fabric took me in, made me feel like melted ice cream, unresisting and formless. On party nights she would bathe and then come into the bedroom she shared with my father, where I would be waiting, perched on their bed, leaning against their pillows at the headboard where I could have a full view of my mother standing in front of the huge mirror above their double dresser. After she had put on her bra, her panties and her garter belt (what a puzzle that piece of clothing seemed) and her silk stockings (I knew the silk were saved for very best. No rayon or lisle for party nights) she would pick up her brush, bend over and toss her waist length hair over her head. She would brush the brown/red length of it for what seemed like an hour and I would not take my eyes off her hand wielding the brush, up to her scalp and down to the very tips of her hair and again, over and over. My own short, brown hair would be like that some day. I knew it, just as I knew I would wear the same blue gown and the same big bangle bracelet and the same shiny black clutch bag that my mother wore for every party, and there were many of them in those days, and in which she looked fresh and beautiful and happy every time.

* * *

God sat on a soft cushion, surrounded by an enormous field of parts. Legs and arms and heads, some with blue eyes and some with brown but none with hair. The hair was in another place, a sort of basket beside God to his right. He worked at a slow, steady pace putting the babies together and wrapping each one in a white blanket. I saw God doing this before I was born, while I was one of the assembled babies waiting to come down to our parents. All of the babies had pink cheeks and very pale white faces and I couldn't tell which were boys and which were girls. I remember telling my mother about what God did to make my brother and me. I thought we were just sharing something that everybody knew but she seemed surprised. She told me that I was the only one she had ever known who had seen God at work.

* * *

The words began with my mother. She read to my brother and me, told us stories, and let us read what we chose. "They'll only understand what they're ready to understand. And they'll learn to ask questions." I remember slogging through Havelock Ellis' "The Dance of Life", at the age of ten. I learned much later that the English psychologist's book was about sex and that it was 'all the rage' for a number of years in the late thirties. To me it was incomprehensible, but the words were there on the page and so they had value and someday I would know what they meant. Edgar Allen Poe and O'Henry and Charles Dickens authored my world for many years. Conan Doyle's Sherlock Holmes and A.A.Milne's Pooh and Mary Travers' Mary Poppins were my friends in that world. They had the advantage of portability. I thought of them as steadfast. Like the steadfast tin soldier, they could be counted on to be there no matter where or how often we moved. My mother played word games with us. Alphabet, in which we were to make up a sentence adding words in turn that began with the letters of the alphabet in order, and each player had to repeat the whole sentence as it grew before adding his word. It was wise to use as many adjectives as possible before settling on a subject noun. "Adorable, beautiful, charming, doddering, Edith, forgot going home . . . ." Sometimes we played using just one letter, seeing how far we could take the sentence. "Beautiful bouncing Betty borrowed Barbara's best brown bag but Bobby . . ." Or my mother would tell me her favorite words and ask me to tell her mine. Hers were the 'm' words, murmuring and morning and mama. Safe, comforting words. Mine were polysyllabic with no regard for beginning letters or for meaning. I loved the way they felt in my mouth and the way they sounded, powerful and crisp. They were the path to being an adult. Paleontology and hydroelectric and legerdemain. And she could recite long, story telling poems from memory. She had taken elocution lessons as a young girl and had won prizes for her public recitations. "Life is a stocking, Grandma said, and I am knitting the toe of mine. My work is almost done." That one, sad and romantic and true, was my favorite. There was one about a conceited jar of strawberry jam which thought itself the only proper offering for the visiting minister's tea and scones, but the jam fretted so over the possibility of being by-passed for the humble raspberry jam that 'she at last fermented' and the raspberry jam was served instead. A lesson in not taking yourself so seriously that you turn sour. I remember watching my mother when she recited and thinking that she was somehow magic to have all those words in her head. The hardest thing, she told me in later years, about having to leave school after her sophomore year to go to work, was the loss of English class, that easy access to books and the company of others who were reading what she read and could talk about it with her. I think she was anxious to have me read so she would have company in the world of words.

My father's words were different. They came from his world as an aviator or from the things he invented or from his hunting deer, and they were purposeful. Not that he did not tell stories. He did. Wild west tales of Pecos Bill or stories of Camelot. Arthur and Gawain and Lancelot. His language was colorful and all the words were right but it was the action, the excitement of his telling that stayed with me more than what he said. What I do remember are the words he used when he talked with my mother or with other men, words like magnetos and pistons and polychokes and altimeters. I didn't need to know what they were or how they worked. It was enough to hear him say the words. To say them myself. And I did begin to learn the meaning of some of them and the names of the people who were important to my father. Igor Sikorsky who was working on something called an autogyro which would become the helicopter. More beautiful words. Alexander DeSeversky, another aviation pioneer. I remember that when my father spoke of Charles Lindbergh it was with quiet respect. Lindbergh had been the first man to fly solo across the Atlantic Ocean and it had happened the year I was born, 1927, so Lindbergh's name had been a part of my very early vocabulary. When I was nine the Lindbergh's infant son was kidnapped and murdered and the name became the sound of an unsafe world. I heard ladders against the wall outside my window, heard the window sliding up, and knew that my parents in their bedroom were too far away to save me. Bruno Hauptmann, the man convicted of the murder, was coming for me. 'Lindbergh' and 'Hauptmann' replaced the words ogre and witch and monster in my mind and made it hard for me to fall asleep. But the good words were compelling and I responded to them by learning all I could of them, using their power to make a safe place in the world for me and for my family. I remember the names of the kinds of planes my father flew. Stearman, Sikorsky amphibian, low wing monoplane, biplane and the Grumman that he flew when he was private pilot for Charles W. Deeds, the Vice-President of Pratt and Whitney Aircraft. That whole string of words that was the answer to the question "What does your father do?" was so sweet that I would say it over and over to myself. It felt like the kind of thing that could never change. Someone could ask me that question when I was a hundred years old and the answer would still be true.

"My father flies a private plane for C. W. Deeds, the Vice-President of Pratt and Whitney Aircraft."

* * *

Saturday morning was cleaning day and as soon as I was big enough to kneel beside the bathtub and reach down into it with a scrubbing rag I staked my claim. All porcelain surfaces were mine. My mother declared the cleaning of all toilets and sinks and tubs and tiles to be my Saturday morning task by divine right. I was the Bab-O Queen. Not that there were other claimants rushing the bathroom door. My brother took out the garbage when he remembered, helped rake the leaves or sweep out the garage and was happy to let me remove soap scum and rust spots from the indoor conveniences. The gleam of a chrome faucet that has been wiped with vinegar and dried with a soft rag to the luster of old silver meant nothing to him.

When I was very small, long before I was part of the household cleaning force, I dragged a chair over to climb up and watch my mother clean the kitchen sink. She was quietly methodical about it, as she was about everything she did around the house. A moderate steady pace with no hurried motions or wasted steps. She would run water in the sink, hold her dish cloth under the running faucet and then turn the water off and wring the cloth between her hands so completely that the knubbly cotton square would be only slightly damp. Then she would shake the can of cleanser so that a thin white coating covered the damp surface of the sink, Bon Ami for the kitchen, Bab-O for the bathroom, I don't know why. Then the best part. I remember her long beautiful fingers working the cloth over the bottom and the sides of the sink and her index finger poking the cloth into each corner. When not one stain remained she would turn the faucet on again and rinse the sink and her dish cloth until all signs of cleanser were gone. Then she would sniff her dish cloth, raise it up to her nose and take a deep breath in. If she was not satisfied that her cloth was sweet she would fill a bowl with water, add baking soda or vinegar and put the cloth to soak. I remember how disgusted she would be if there was the slightest hint of mildew. A sour dishcloth was the sign of a poor housekeeper and, I think now, hinted at other failings. What delighted me was the completeness of her work. "Good enough" was never good enough. When I took over the cleaning of the bathroom it was with the certainty that I would leave the fixtures as bright as my mother's kitchen sink. I remember being totally successful. If the truth was something less than that, she never said.

* * *

The food of my childhood was filling and satisfying. My mother called herself a "good plain cook" and that seems right. Potatoes and soups and stews and pot roasts, flavorful and steaming, served to us, my father and my brother and me, by my mother, her face flushed from the heat of the stove and her eyes on my father's face. "Is it good?' "Does it need salt?' "Is it hot enough?" The three of us would be eating before she had her apron off and was seated opposite my father.

One of my favorite meals was scalloped potatoes, perhaps because it was a simple dish and I could help with the preparation. From my usual vantage point standing on a kitchen chair pulled up to the counter or to the enamel pull-out shelf of the Hoosier cabinet, I would watch my mother peel a bag of potatoes. She held the green wooden handle of the peeler so easily in her curled fingers. The sharp curved blade moved over the surface of the potato, the long thin brown skin, nearly always in one piece, fell onto the brown paper bag my mother had flattened on the counter to receive what would be garbage but what looked like dusty ribbons piling up as she worked. She would hand each potato to me and I would put it into the bowl filled with salted water that stood on the counter in front of me. "To keep them from turning brown, Shirley. They look so much more appetizing when they keep their color." When she had gathered up the peels and thrown them away, she would slice the potatoes, thin and even, her hands moving like a machine. I would be given a torn scrap of brown paper with which to grease the casserole into which the potatoes would be placed. I loved this part of the preparation, scrunching the bit of paper, dipping it into the open can of Crisco and scooping up the white lard, spreading it over the bottom and sides of the Pyrex oven dish. We would place the potato slices over the bottom of the pan, carefully, as if we were making a mosaic, sprinkling each layer with salt and pepper and a dusting of flour. Then I would cut bits from the oblong pound of sweet fresh butter from the dairy and place them evenly over the layer of potatoes. My mother would get a bottle of milk from the ice box and pour just until the milk showed between the potatoes on the top layer. Sometimes there was ham to be sliced and added between the layers, which made a good dish perfection. When the scalloped potatoes reached the table after their time in the oven the top was a bubbling brown crust and the aroma made me weak in the knees.

 My father and I shared bedtime food of his choosing. Shredded Wheat, two biscuits each in deep soup bowls, covered with cream which was poured over the biscuits and allowed to soak in before the biscuit was broken into bite sized pieces with the side of a soup spoon. Sugar was then sprinkled over the whole, the grains sparkling like new snow on the mounds of Shredded Wheat. We would sit at the kitchen table to enjoy the full pleasure of the crisp cereal and the smooth, thick cream. The other choice for pre-bed eating was a sandwich of peanut butter on Wonder Bread with Hellman's Mayonnaise and a whole ripe banana sliced over the peanut butter. This was not snacking. This was eating. I don't remember the word 'snacking' from my childhood. Others may have used it but in my family we 'ate' at what ever hour the food was consumed. I don't remember any conversation with my father during these night sessions. We did not use the time to go over our day nor did we share confidences. We were there to enjoy the food and each other's silent company and enjoy we did.

If there was not great variety in our meals, they were always prepared with care and as much inventiveness as the supply of food allowed. Vegetables and fruits were entirely seasonal so my mother used canned foods to supplement our diet. I preferred canned peas to fresh and canned peaches to those just off the tree. We had root vegetables all winter, carrots and potatoes and parsnips, which I loved. And apples lasted most of the winter, whether held in the basement by my mother or in warehouses by the retail grocers. There were no super-markets, but the small owner-run shops provided good food and wonderful service. If you couldn't get to the store you could telephone your order in the morning and it would be delivered that afternoon. No charge.

And then there was food that was so exotic that I didn't expect to eat it in my lifetime. In fact, I thought I probably wouldn't want to try it, wouldn't like it. Shrimp and oysters and caviar and Charlotte russe and lobster. But my father had catholic tastes in food as he did in people so eventually I tried them all. All but the oysters and the lobster became favorites. He took us to Chinese restaurants and to hotel restaurants and to malt shops and to hamburger stands. That we ate in restaurants at all set us apart from any of my friends. Adults ate meals out but children did so very seldom if at all. I remember how it felt to be waited on by a man in a white jacket and black pants or a woman in a black dress and white apron whose only job was to see that I had everything I wanted. Set apart and like a princess, having all this attention and having done nothing to deserve it. I loved it. My father encouraged my mother to try making Mexican food. They had taken a trip to California and had been excited by the tastes they had found in the food there. My mother's chili, which she served at their parties, was the first most of their friends had ever tasted. They loved it and my brother and I loved it. She served it with Saltines and a split banana to cut the heat of the chili powder. And she toasted the caraway seeds in an iron frying pan, carefully watched so they didn't burn. She said it was the secret of good chili.

I remember corn bread, a huge flat pan of it, enough to feed ten or twelve at Nana's table. My father's mother, Nana, had a cook, an Irish woman named Sarah Morrow who had come to live at the farm when she was sixteen. She was gray haired and slow and almost toothless by the time I remember her and she made the best cornbread I ever ate. She called me Sunshine and she let me help her in the kitchen whenever I wanted. She gave each of Nana's many grandchildren a 'bakery' birthday cake on their special day, as if her own efforts in the baking department couldn't possibly be good enough for us. Sarah didn't leave the house. Saint Patrick had chased all the snakes out of Ireland and they were waiting for her outside the back door. She would fling the washed dish towels over the bushes just outside the door to dry. The priest brought Communion to her. She wanted for nothing she said and I believed her.

My mother's mother was the source of sweets and goodies. She had helped to support her four children by making candies at one time in her life and the touch never left her. Snow or rain would begin to fall past the kitchen windows and she would say, "Let's make fudge" or someone in the family would be feeling under the weather and she would say, "A batch of popcorn'll set you right" or company would be coming and she would say "I think penuche would be good, don't you?" Penuche would be wonderful. Sometimes the treat to be prepared depended on what was in the house. If there was no sugar we made popcorn. If there was no Baker's Chocolate we made fondant. But Grandma always made it seem as if that was just what we had wanted to make all along. For weeks before Christmas she would make mint fondants and dip them in chocolate, double batches of fudge, Chinese Chew by the dozens. Chinese Chew was a combination of dried dates and figs and coconut and dried red and green cherries and whatever nuts were at hand. Pecans were the best. She would put everything in a huge kettle and mix it with a long wooden spoon and then we would sit together, Grandma and whoever else was at home, cousins, my uncle, my aunt, and form the Chinese Chew into balls and then roll each ball in granulated sugar before wrapping it in waxed paper and twisting the ends of the paper to seal the candy in.

In the midst of the Great Depression and then through the long years of The War solid satisfying meals were continuity and reassurance. Food was love and caring and safety. Taste and selective eating and the enjoyment of haute cuisine came later, in a time of plenty, and never tasted as good as scalloped potatoes fresh from the oven.

* * *

My mother and I did not look alike. Her skin was darker and her brown hair had red lights in it. Her fingers were thin and her hands moved through the air like birds. She wore the brightest red nail polish Cutex made. I thought her fingers ended in a point. Mine were blunt, like my father's. Not that I looked like him. Just that there were some things about him that were familiar to me. His pale skin that freckled in the summer. His big-toothed grin. I could see those things repeated in me. Nothing of my mother showed up no matter how hard I looked. Her eyes were large and her brows were perfect arches over them. My eyes looked squinty to me and my brows were wide and thin. I remember thinking that my mother was beauty and I was something else. I wasn't malformed or scary or anything. Just not beauty.

    She would sit at the kitchen table with a cup of coffee in front of her, a lighted cigarette between the first two fingers of her right hand, her thumb tapping at the tobacco at the bottom of the cigarette, taking a long slow drag on the unfiltered tube at regular intervals, looking to me like a goddess performing a ritual I might someday be trusted to learn. The things she kept in her purse and it was always called a purse, not a pocketbook or a bag, were further proof of her position as a goddess in my world. The keys and the golden compact with its perfect mirror on the inside of its perfect lid, the slender lipstick in its swivel case, the packet of Luckies with its cellophane wrapper, smooth and cool to the touch and the shiny tin foil ragged at the top where my mother had torn it open, the worn tan leather wallet with real money in its thin pocket and the coins at the bottom of the purse, in that dark narrow crease where the shreds of tobacco and a single spearmint Chiclet lived. She was generous with her amulets. I could dump the contents of her purse onto the candlewick bedspread on the big mahogany double bed where she and my father slept and where he fought his asthma with the tank of oxygen standing just to the left of the headboard and where he read the funnies to my brother and me on some special Sunday mornings.

    I would jingle her keys, try them in the never locked lock of the bedroom door, imagine sliding the odd shaped key into the ignition of whatever car we had at the moment and then turn my attention to her makeup. I remember opening her compact, pushing in on the tiny clasp and hearing the satisfying click, watching the lid pop up and then looking at myself in the small round polished metal mirror. I would pick up the lipstick, open it and twist the bottom until the waxy red stick emerged, slide the red over my mouth, pinching my lips together to spread the color the way my mother always did and each time I did it feeling that that single moment was the happiest of my life.

I was allowed to play with her jewelry box, too. More charms and symbols of her power. A wide green bracelet of Bakelite backed with a copper colored metal. Looking through the curved glass-like material I could see an ocean or a forest or a fairy glade. It was so much too big for me that I usually settled for carrying it around the room peering through it as if through a kaleidoscope. And there was a jeweled comb that she wore in her hair when she and my father went to very special parties. I knew I would never wear that comb in my thin, lank hair, but I could wear a ring on every finger and drape her necklaces around my neck and feel that much closer to inheriting my mother's magic.

* * *

The first escalator in Hartford was installed at Kresge's, my grandmother's favorite 'five and dime'. Grandma Rough and I would plan our trips to Hartford carefully, gathering what coins we could over time, the minimum being a quarter each, and we would take the trolley into town. The ride cost a nickel each way and the extra fifteen cents would enable us to have lunch at White Tower. Occasionally my grandmother had a crumpled dollar or even two in her coin purse which we would spend at Kresge's. Ten cents for a Cutex lipstick, the tiny one with the delicate point in a case that did not swivel. A lace hankie with an initial M embroidered delicately in one corner to put away for Aunt Martha for Christmas. Once we bought a small vial of Blue Waltz perfume for my mother. It came in a blue bottle and was the most extravagant gift I could imagine. A present that wasn't to be worn or saved for best or anything. Just to make you smell delicious. And then, if there was any change left over, we would buy a dozen of the doughnuts that were made in the wonderful machine in the front window of the store, six plain, six sugared, in a white paper bag that I held in my lap on the way home. There would be grease stains on my coat and two fewer doughnuts in the bag by the time we walked in the front door at home.

One Saturday Grandma took me to the top of Kresge's escalator (it ran between the first floor and the basement) and said, "Let's try it. I want to look at the mark-downs. Maybe get a sweater for Rink."

I remember looking down the long wooden stairs, clattering and clanking as they rolled away from where we stood, each step appearing from some unseen place that sounded of machinery, wheels and cogs and grinding plates that would grab an unwary or unbalanced foot and pull the owner of such a foot into its jaws to be chewed up and spit out. Try it? I thought not. Not for any reason would I get on those slotted, undulating, unsafe steps. And I didn't want my grandmother to try it either. How would I get home alone? What could I say to my mother? "Grandma was eaten by the Kresge's escalator."

"I can't, Gram. I'm scared of it," I said.

"Well, then, you'll have to stand right here. Right here," she said again, pointing with the toe of her black oxford to show me exactly what square foot of tiled floor I was to occupy while she went to look over the bargains in the basement. "Don't move and don't talk to strangers, honey. I'll be quick."

And she grabbed the moving rail at the side of the stairs and stepped onto the first stair that emerged. She teetered and grabbed at the opposite rail with her other hand and sailed off down the escalator, getting farther and farther from me until I watched her step off at the bottom, turn to wave and smile reassurance up at me. The woman on the step behind her bumped into her and they went off together laughing. The experience of riding on a moving stairway was new and I could see people were enjoying it, calling out to one another, laughing the way my grandma had laughed. I didn't care. Elevators were bad enough. I hadn't been in many of those, either, but at least the floor didn't give way under your feet.

Time went by. Hours, I thought. I couldn't see my grandma anywhere among the people passing at the foot of the escalator. Where is she? Has something happened to her? Grandma Rough was the source of every horror story of my childhood. She knew of children who had been carried off by seemingly helpful, decent, strangers. Little boys who had had their limbs severed by passing vehicles. "Do not lean out of the window in a car or in a trolley. A passing truck will decapitate you." Not could, but will. Little girls who had had something done to them that even she could not talk about and by neighbors, people the little girls had been told to watch out for. What might happen to an elderly lady in the basement of a crowded dime store? I imagined abduction and eventual murder at the hands of a deranged shopper. Where was my grandmother?

I was standing on my designated tile, crying, when a large, gray-haired black woman came to stand in front of me, bending to speak. "What is it, honey? Are you lost? Where's your mommy?"

She looked like a grandmother to me. Her brown winter coat and her black felt hat were familiar, like my grandma's. Instantly she was not a stranger, she was help when I needed it most.

"My grandma's down there," I said, sobbing, pointing down the escalator to the bargain basement.

"Well, let's go find her," she said, putting out her hand.

I took her hand, stepped beside her onto the escalator and descended to the basement as if on a magic carpet. Even the rumbling of the stairs under my feet didn't scare me. The woman's big, warm hand was wrapped around mine so closely that there was no room for fear. Grandma Rough was approaching the up escalator as we came down.

"What's this, Shirley? I wasn't gone long. Are you all right?" My grandma sounded anxious, as if I had been the one in danger there at the top of the stairs.

"Your little granddaughter was just getting lonesome for you. She's a really brave little girl," the woman said.

"Well, I thank you so much for bringing her down. She didn't want any part of moving stairs, but I guess you have a way with you. Thanks, again."

My grandmother reached out and put her hand on the woman's arm and they grinned at each other before each turned to go her own way. Grandma and I stepped onto the up escalator as if we had always done it just that way. It wasn't until we were sitting on the slippery rattan seat of the trolley that I realized I hadn't said my own thank you. Grandma and I were the first ones in our family to ride on an escalator and the only way I could have done it was to speak to a stranger, to go with a stranger. I remember wondering what my mother would say when we told her what I had done.

"The exceptions only prove the rule. You were lucky such a nice woman found you," she said. "Don't do it again."

I didn't. A stranger was a stranger and a savior was a savior. I would not mistake the one for the other.

* * *

The grown-ups in my life were busy with their own things. My father was flying, as far removed from us as he could be, in the clouds or skimming tree tops or carrying important people to important places. My mother was tending the house, cleaning or shopping for food or sewing, and sometimes playing bridge with her friends or getting her hair 'permed', though that wasn't often. She had cut her long hair to a fashionable short bob. She was still beautiful but now she had to sit under a monster machine in the beauty parlor every six months or so and have huge clamps that were attached by wire to a monster machine attached to her head. She looked frizzy when she came home and my father would tease her about her tomboy cut. Most of the time she was there in the house and we were allowed to play outdoors by ourselves as long as we didn't roam too far. I don't remember any feeling of her eyes on us or of her peeking through the curtains to be sure we weren't 'acting up'. Some of our friends had that kind of mother and I remember what a feeling of guilt I had when we played at their houses. I must be doing something really bad for Billy's mommy to be always coming out on the porch, calling to us, "You kids stay away from that road, you hear me?" We weren't near the road. Wouldn't be near the road. The occasional cars whizzing past at twenty-five or thirty miles an hour, as my father had told me they did, were threat enough. I could feel my body recoil at the thought of being hit by one of them. Still I was guilty of something. Betty's mother would invite me in to play with her daughter who was a year older than I. She would tell us to go up to Betty's room and then she would walk past the open door of the bedroom fifty times an hour. She would carry the laundry from room to room or move a dust mop along the hall floor or just walk past, humming under her breath as if she had business somewhere down the hall of that tiny house. Betty and I would play tea party with her beautiful china tea set, but Betty would always pour. "I have to be really careful of this china. My aunt gave it to me and you might chip it or something." Guilty. Of course I would have chipped it. I never doubted it for a moment. Betty always wanted to play at our house. "Your mother is so much fun," she would say. My mother didn't play with us but she took time to visit with

Betty, with any of our friends who came to play. "How is your mother? And how's that wicked cat of yours?" my mother would say and Betty would laugh out loud. Betty's cat was a stuffed toy that sat on her bed and was never played with. My mother let Betty think she thought it was a real cat, too wild, too exotic for ordinary play.

Betty and I and my brother if he was around, would take the tins of real food that my mother let us have from her pantry, line them up on the top step of the back porch and play store. No adult taught us how or what to play. The grownups were busy with their own things and they let us be busy with ours.

* * *

The man who raised pigeons lived on a farm on a back road that was hardly a road. A narrow, unlit dirt lane that branched off onto a rutted sand track led to his house and barn. I went there with my father when my mother wanted squab for a special dinner. The man and my father would talk, standing outside on the patch of grass that was the lawn for the gray shingle house. There were no flowers, no color at all that I remember. They would puff on their pipes and say things like, "Sorry weather" and "Too bad about your truck" and finally, "How many birds do ya' need, Jimmy?" and my father would say "Oh, four'll do this time", making it sound as if he sometimes bought twenty. He nearly always bought four, never more than six. The man, small and gray himself like his house, would walk off to the side of the barn where the cotes were, the sheds that held the pigeons, and my father would follow him, swinging his trousered wooden leg to clear the rough grass. They said nothing to my brother or me. We sat in the car and waited for our father to come back with the brown paper wrapped package in his two hands. He would put it on the floor in the back seat and tell my brother, "Toddy, don't put your feet on the package.

That's dinner for Sunday." I don't remember how much money he gave the man for the squab but I do remember him saying as we drove away, "That'll be dinner for them, too, for a week of Sundays."

I didn't know who he meant by *them*. I thought the man lived alone out there on that dark ugly farm, but one evening, about a week before Halloween, we all rode out to the pigeon farm. My mother had never been there and she asked a lot of questions as we drove.

"What's his wife like? Should we have brought something as a house gift? How old is the little boy?"

I hadn't known there was a boy. My father just kept driving, looking straight ahead and saying little. "They're nice people, Bertie." and, just as we drove up to the house, he stopped the car and put out the headlights. "The boy's about eight, I think. Maybe seven. Little thing." Younger than I, older than Todd. A light went on in a front room and then the man opened the door onto the porch.

"That you, Jimmy? Come on in," he called.

We got out of the car and walked up the two steps to the porch. The splintery, gray wood looked like it wouldn't hold all four of us. I held back and waited till my mother and father were safely in the door before I put my foot on the porch. Todd had waited, too. He followed me.

"Where's the kids, Jimmy? Didn't ya bring the kids?" I heard the man say, sounding really disappointed, as if he had been waiting for us. That was nice. It made me feel less shy about going into the house, meeting his wife and little boy.

We walked into the front room, no entry, no hall, just right into the parlor. It was as tan and brown a room as the house on the outside was gray. The wallpaper was tan with huge tan fern like leaves printed on it. The paper was peeling away from the wall in places and the wall underneath had been painted a tannish yellow. There was a big brown couch that looked lumpy and worn, not like our nice blue couch at home. One chair upholstered in the same brown as the couch was against one wall and two wooden chairs, one of them a rocker, were opposite the couch. There was one standing lamp with a parchment shade and a pair of sconces on the wall on either side of the fireplace. They were all turned on but I remember how dark the room seemed to me. The man's wife came in from the kitchen carrying a tray of glasses and a pitcher of lemonade.

"I'm so glad you all could come. I've been wanting to meet you," she said as she put the tray on an upended box the man had slid in front of the couch. "Pardon us. We don't have anything very grand," she said. She was small and bright and she looked happy, smiling all the while she poured lemonade for all of us. I wondered where the boy was.

"Freddy's been so excited all day. I let him stay home from school so he could get ready for tonight," the woman said. I liked her right away. She let her little boy stay home from school and he wasn't even sick.

"Fred, come on down now. Company's here," the man called out, standing at the door into the kitchen.

Freddy came into the room so quietly that I remember being startled to look up and see him. He was small, no taller than Todd, and thin and he looked scared. He had his hands behind his back and he smiled a tight smile at Todd and me.

"Freddy's been planning a kind of Halloween party if that's all right with you," the woman said to my mother. "He doesn't have friends way out here in the country the way we are, so we thought . . ." she said, looking over at Todd and me.

"What a good idea," my mother said.

I could tell by the way she said it that Todd and I had better cooperate, had better have a good time with Freddy. Our best manners were being called on. Freddy brought his hands around to the front to show us the paper masks he'd been hiding. They were the black eye masks that you could get at the dime store, the ones with the elastic to hold them on. No goblins or ghosts or witches. Just plain black masks. We each took one and put it on. Todd and I followed Freddy into the dark kitchen and on into the two other rooms downstairs. No lights at all and I was scared. I had to follow the sound of Freddy's footsteps in this unfamiliar place. I hadn't thought to take Todd's hand so I didn't know if he was ahead or behind. When Freddy opened the kitchen door, I could see Todd outlined for a minute, then all three of us were running outside as fast as we could, across the nearly pitch black yard and around and around the barn. We shrieked and yelled and hollered, scaring each other and ourselves, falling down, scraping our knees in the dirt, getting up and running on. I was surprised to hear my father's voice calling us. "Come on, kids. It's time to go home." It seemed we'd been playing only minutes. We ran to the car and climbed into the back seat. Freddy's mother leaned into the passenger side front window.

"Nice of you kids to join in like you did. It meant the world to Freddy."

We hadn't talked with Freddy at all, just screamed and shrieked and run till we were breathless, but he had given us a wonderful Halloween party and we were sorry to have it end.

A few weeks later we came again for squab and it was like all the times before. Our father went into the barn with Freddy's father and came back with the brown paper package, got into the car and that was that. We hadn't seen anything of Freddy or his mother. I was shy about speaking without being spoken to, but I did say in my most polite voice, "Say hi to Freddy". He didn't answer but he waved as we drove off. I asked my father why Freddy and his family didn't talk much.

"They talk enough to get by," was all he said.

We never saw Freddy again. When my mother reminded me of that night, "Wasn't that fun? Such a nice family," I couldn't answer her. The thought of it, of Freddy with his dime store masks and no candy corn and no going out for trick or treat and what his mother said, no friends, just made me want to cry. All the excitement of the night was gone and I was left feeling sorry that I couldn't do anything to change things for Freddy.

In time I would understand that Freddy's life, impoverished of material things and isolated by circumstance, no family car, no telephone, no near neighbors, was simply his life and that his parents knew how to help him celebrate the smallest pleasure, how to share what he had with anyone willing to join in the fun. In the same way our mother encouraged my brother and me in the appreciation of the little joys, a stick of gum from our father's jacket pocket, the taste of the bark of a black birch tree, a trip to our grandmother's for the day.

She was right, Halloween had been fun for us and fun for Freddy. But I knew what I knew and nothing made the guilt of having more than someone as small and generous as Freddy go away.

* * *

We ate a lot of sandwiches in summer, tuna fish and peanut butter and home made grape jelly, so my mother wouldn't have to fire up the stove until near supper time. We had electric fans but they didn't do much more than move the humid summer air around in lazy circles. My grandmother used to place a bowl of ice in front of the fan to 'cool the air'. It made you think you were cooler for a few minutes. I remember her getting up very early on the worst of the dog days. She would fill a bucket with water, take it out to the front porch and heave it onto the cement floor where it would splash and run and puddle on the already hot surface. Steam rose as she swept the water into every corner of the porch with her kitchen broom. I don't remember her having a new broom, ever. I'm sure she did, but the ones I remember were worn to a slant with sweeping and they shed bristles as she swept. The loose bristles were kept in a glass in the Hoosier cabinet for testing cakes for doneness.

Hoosier cabinets took pride of place in the kitchen of any woman lucky enough to have one. They were wonders of efficiency and, I thought, of beauty. The cabinet was built with double doors for storage on the bottom half. An enameled shelf that could be slid out for rolling pastry covered the top of the bottom half. The top half was set back about two thirds of the way and consisted of a set of double doors hiding shelves on the right. Below the shelves was a carousel holding condiment containers, glass jars with metal perforated tops. A big metal flour bin was set behind the single door on the left. There was a mica window in the bin so that the cook could see how much flour she had left and the bottom of the bin was a sifter. Some had tip out bins in the bottom half as well, for sugar and root vegetables. Most of the cabinets were oak and were left unpainted, but I remember at least one that had been painted the green that in the thirties seemed to be the only color allowed in kitchens. I remember pulling a chair over to the Hoosier and helping my mother roll out pie dough. She would let me have the scraps to sprinkle with cinnamon and sugar from one of the glass jars in the carousel. I would roll the dough into pin wheels, my mother would slice it into beautiful little cookies and bake them along with her pie in the big, dark oven of the iron stove. I would snatch up a cookie from the cooling rack, burn my tongue on the hot sugar, take a swallow of cold milk, and go back for another cookie.

In one or two houses we had refrigerators. We called all of them Frigidaires no matter who made them. One was a Westinghouse, I remember, with the motor on the outside of the refrigerator, set right up on top. It was circular and had a grid of metal around it. More often we had ice boxes, those brown wooden cabinets that held a block of ice behind one door and storage space for food behind the other. A zinc tray slid under the ice box to catch the drips as the ice melted. The tray had to be emptied at least once a day. The ice man with his horse drawn cart full of huge blocks of ice would turn into our street and we could hear the horses hooves on the paved street two blocks away. I would grab a brown paper bag and hurry down to the curb where nearly always other children would be waiting. We would tear a piece of brown Kraft paper from the grocery bag, make a cone of it and hold it up, waiting for the slivers and shavings of ice the ice man would scoop into it. We watched him wield his murderous looking ice pick, shaping a small block of ice from one of the big ones resting in sawdust on the bed of his wagon, whittling it to the size our mother had indicated she needed. The mothers on the block placed a pasteboard sign in their windows. The large black numbers printed on the sign told him what size chunk of ice was wanted, 10LBS, 25 LBS, 50 LBS. We sat on the curb sucking on our frigid treats and watched him heft the block of ice with his huge tongs, hang it from his scale, hardly looking at the number on the dial, (we knew that he knew he had cut 25 lbs.) and then fling it up where it would ride on the square of leather he wore on his shoulder to keep himself dry. He wore a water spotted leather apron, too, and I thought he was beautiful. It was what he did that pleased my heart, moving so surely, using his tools with precision. And his generosity of spirit, too, I found irresistible. There were jokes I was too young to understand about the visits of the ice man, but I thought it only right that there be laughter when my ice man was mentioned.

We had indoor plumbing for the most part, though some of my relatives in Michigan did not. No such thing as a shower, though, and I really wanted a shower. It seemed like such a wonderful thing. You'd feel like you were out in the rain without your clothes on and I knew what that felt like. My mother let us, my brother and me, run naked in the rain when we were at our summer cabin. There was no one around for miles and we were allowed great freedom. A shower indoors seemed like a year round possibility for that same feeling. It would not be until I was ten and we moved into our own home, a house my father had built for us, that we had a shower. It was only a small let down. Not quite running naked in the rain but wonderful for washing my hair without having to stand over the sink.

We camped every summer, sometimes in tents and sometimes in a trailer my father and grandfather had built, and the camp sites we stayed at in those days had only what were called privies for toilets. One, two, or three hole wooden sheds, foul smelling and unlit. The planks with the holes cut into them for sitting on were often rough and were always unpainted. Splinters were not only possible but probable and the ignominy of having a sliver tweezed from my bare bottom was one of the many things that made camping a less than ideal way to spend the summer, at least to me. The toilet paper in these rustic communal bathrooms was waxy, tough, scarce and ineffective. My mother carried rolls of toilet paper with us so we could have a bit of comfort. I had a horror of any privy because of the spiders that were going to attack me from below as soon as I settled on the scratchy seat. How on earth could one protect oneself from the wildlife that teemed in those black, stinking holes? My mother finally found an old bucket which we kept at the campsite, used as needed and emptied as necessary. No porcelain toilet was ever more appreciated than that bucket. The idea that a spider might make a home as easily in the bucket as in the privy didn't occur to me.

I remember our radios, either a large wooden cabinet with a green-lit dial on its face and a fabric covered speaker in its belly or a smaller Bakelite or wooden table model often in the shape of a Gothic window. My mother and I loved the soap operas, called serials. "Helen Trent" and "One Man's Family" and "Ma Perkins". After school, my brother and I would tune in "I Love a Mystery" and "Jack Armstrong, the All-American Boy" and "The Lone Ranger." In the evenings and on week-ends my father joined us in the living room where we sat around the Stromberg-Carlson watching the lighted dial and and listening to Jack Benny, Fibber McGee and Molly, Fred Allen and Allen's Alley, and Amos and Andy. We listened to President Roosevelt's fireside chats, my brother and I getting what we could from his talks. His voice was rich and warm. Mostly intimate, sometimes exhorting. All of the people who spoke to us over the air waves became familiar friends. I could name the actors who played the parts, Olan Soule and Barbara Luddy on Lux Radio Theater, Mason Adams as Pepper Young and all the others. I discovered my mother's sense of humor, her adult sense of humor, when she and I began listening to two fifteen minute programs that came on in the middle of the day just as I got home from school for lunch. "Frank Watanabe and the Honorable Archy" and "Batiste Himself from Canada". This was humor with an edge, ethnic and aimed at an adult audience. One dealt with a Japanese gardener who was smarter than his employer and the other a French Canadian who used his accent to make us laugh, not at him but with him. My mother and I would eat our bowl of Campbell's Tomato Soup and Saltines in silence, except for our shared laughter. Later in our lives, after my father had died and my mother and I were sharing a bedroom on the chilly third floor of my Nana's house, she and I found Henry Morgan and Victor Borge on the radio. We would huddle together under the blankets and laugh at these two dry, witty, outrageous men. The first laughter, and as it turned out, the only laughter that I heard from my mother for a long dark time. Everyone listened to the radio. Everyone could tell you what George Burns had said to Gracie Allen the night before. I heard my first classical music on the radio, heard the news that we were going to war on the radio, heard people reading poetry and acting in Shakespearean plays on the radio. Radio was classless. And it was safe. There would be no blue language surprising you in the middle of your favorite show. And best of all, in a time when "Brother Can You Spare a Dime" replaced the national anthem as our collective theme song, it was free.

My mother called the wicker baby carriage I pushed my baby brother around in a 'baby buggy' It could be converted into a stroller as the baby became a toddler. A section of the bottom of the carriage nearest the head could be pushed up and latched to provide a back rest for the child. The foot section of the carriage could be released and dropped down to make a place for the child's feet. I don't remember strollers as separate entities from carriages in the thirties, though they may well have existed. The carriages which were shiny black or navy and which rode high on bright metal springs and had folding canvas hoods that could be opened to protect the baby from sun or rain were called perambulators or prams. They were often imported from England and they carried a certain cache. My mother would show me a picture of myself in such a pram and she would smile with pride, more at the carriage than at her baby daughter. "What a beautiful pram. Just look how high it rode." What happened to it, why my baby brother never rode in it, I can't imagine, but I had a feeling of having been privileged at an early age. when I looked at that black and white Kodak. A shiny pram with its coiled springs and its slender lines was no 'baby buggy'.

* * *

I was two years old when I started spending Saturdays at the movies. My teen-aged uncle, who lived with us while he was going to high school, would hoist me to his shoulders and we would go off fo the local theater. I remember sitting on his knees in the dark, sharing popcorn from a big cardboard cup, our fingers greasy with real butter. Sometimes he put me on the edge of the turned up seat next to him but I didn't like the feel of the plush against the back of my knees so he would take me back to his lap. The moment the lights went down and the ushers went to stand in the back at the top of the aisles where they could watch for boys sneaking smokes, that moment was almost too tense with excitement for me to bear it. When the screen in front of us, above us, went from gray to black and white and the rooster or the lion or the globe appeared accompanied by music, my heart would rise beating in my throat and my eyes would lock onto the moving forms before me. I loved the cowboys, handsome, white haired William Boyd as Hop-a-Long Cassidy, and later, Gary Cooper. Their ten gallon hats were white and they rose high in the air so you could find your hero even in the dust of a stampede. There were funny men and women, Zasu Pitts and Marjorie Main, Laurel and Hardy and the Ritz brothers. I laughed at them but I didn't want to be like them. I didn't want to know them the way I wanted to know Richard Greene with his English accent and his dimples or Clark Gable with his deep, almost raspy voice and his smile. At six or eight or ten I felt their attraction and I had fantasy conversations with them, chance encounters of the imagination where I was Claudette Colbert or my absolute heroine, Rosalind Russell. Movie women took on the men and often bested them at the games they all played. Katherine Hepburn and Susan Hayward and Barbara Stanwyck. I took their smart aleck remarks and their jaunty hats and their sense of their own importance and I made an internal model of it all, a template for future reference. The movies were where I found the stories I needed and the people to live them and, most of all, the knowledge that life could be bigger than Girl Scout oxfords and oatmeal and the smell of medicine in the house.

* * *

They came to our house, knocking sometimes on the front door and more often on the back. The Fuller Brush man, the woman with an encyclopedia to sell, our grocery delivery boy, the coal man, the Traveler's Insurance agent, the landlord collecting the rent, the man who sharpened knives and scissors, the paper boy, the poor. We came to know the Fuller Brush man. He showed up at regular intervals with his suitcase full of what he described as 'indispensable household cleaning items'. My mother always asked him in. She might need a whisk broom or a tin of wax, but usually her household budget would tell her she needed nothing. It was neighborly, polite, to ask him in, to offer him a glass of water or lemonade and it provided a break in the day's activities, the dusting and ironing and scrubbing and sweeping and laundering and cooking that occupied my mother's time. The things he offered for sale were the things with which she was most familiar. They would talk about the merits of dry mopping rather than sweeping the parquet floors of our rented house, of paste as preferable to liquid wax on mahogany furniture suites. And they would talk about the economy. How was he doing in this time of no money and few jobs? He was grateful to have employment and people could always find enough change in the bottom of their pockets or in their pin money jars to buy something, any small thing from him. The nickels and dimes kept him and his wife and child from having to live with her parents in Wisconsin and the customer had the thrill of something new, a packet of dust cloths or a vegetable brush. "It works out just fine, thank you for asking, Mrs. Williams. See you in a month. You make a swell glass of lemonade."

* * *

"We'll go to Grandma Rough's on Christmas Eve and to Nana's for Christmas dinner. That'll give us time for our own tree and gifts and stockings on Christmas morning," my mother would say, her voice rising at the end of each sentence as if to encourage us to be happy with what had been decided. Every year she and my father would have a discussion about how to divide the Christmas festivities between their families. They called it a discussion but it was really a fight. I remember their voices raised and angry.

"We always go to the farm for dinner. What's wrong with going to my mother's for once? We can see your mother on Christmas Eve for Pete's sake," my mother would say sounding like she was going to cry.

"Don't you start the water works, Bertie. You know how much Mother counts on all of us being there for the big do. My God, everybody will be there. I'm not going to be the one to disappoint her."

I don't remember a Christmas in those early years that did not turn out exactly as my father wanted it. Christmas Eve at Grandma Rough's with my aunt and uncle and my two cousins, my brother, my parents and me, and always friends dropping in for a cup of eggnog and carols around the player piano. Uncle Rink would have chopped down and brought home a tree and there would be tinsel and lights and ornaments shining on it. We would have food and laughter and candy canes and gifts. The gifts were simple, handkerchiefs, gloves, scarves, a sparkley pin from Woolworth's, socks or ties for the men and everybody always said, "Just what I wanted" no matter what they'd hoped for. What I really wanted was just once to have Christmas Day at Grandma Rough's.

Christmas Day at the farm where the "everybody" my father said would be there meant eight or ten aunts and uncles, more than a dozen cousins, a couple of great aunts,

Nana and Grampa, and other of their guests, some of whom I did not know. There would be a nine foot tree decorated with blown glass birds and fruits that my mother told me were 'imported' and what I thought must be a thousand lights. After a dinner that lasted most of the afternoon, turkey carved by Grampa, mashed potatoes, stuffing and gravy and four or five vegetables, pies for dessert and red and green Jordan almonds in a cut glass dish on the serpentine side board, after all that and just when the anticipation became unbearable, we would go into the double living room and have our gifts. Santa would stomp up onto the wooden front porch, jangling reindeer bells, ho-hoing and carrying a huge sack over his shoulder. One of the older cousins would whisper that Santa was Uncle Jim or Uncle Bill but I knew better. It was Santa. It took a long evening to distribute the gifts to so many children, dolls and trucks and jigsaw puzzles, and at the end Santa reaching into the branches of the tree to find the envelopes of money, our gift from our Greataunt Nan. I remember getting a five dollar bill, the most money I had ever had at one time.

Christmas at Nana's was exciting and exhausting. My brother and I would be asleep in the back seat of the car by the time we got home and I would forget until the next year the thing I knew as surely as I knew anything, that my Grandma Rough had wanted us to be with her for Christmas day and that we never would be.

* * *

My father slept with a gun under his pillow. The gun took the place of his leg. His real leg. His make believe leg, the one he wore during the day, the one people called his wooden leg, stood against the wall in the bedroom he shared with my mother. Close enough for him to reach in the morning, but of no use to him until he strapped it on. The gun was to protect us all in case a burglar broke into the house in the night and found my father helpless in his bed, his good leg inadequate for hopping after robbers. His make believe leg was not a wooden leg. It was a complicated structure of metal and leather and a compound that was the color of flesh but was cold and hard. His foot was made of wood, hinged at the ankle and the metatarsal. It looked like the shoe lasts I had seen in cobbler's shops, the toes all one delicate, thin, pointed oval of wood, connected to the carved, arched main part of the foot by a metal hinge. He wore what he called a sock on the stump of his leg. It was a white woolen tube that was meant to keep the leather straps from chafing, but I had seen him rub at the stump when he took his leg off at night and I knew it didn't do much good. He would put the stump with its sock into the cup-like place at the top of his make believe leg and pull the straps tight, one this way and one that way. He would grunt as he did it, just to make sure everything was as secure as could be. Then he'd pull his trousers up over that leg first and then his real leg. When he stood, it would take him a minute to get his balance. Once he was set, he would walk off like any other father. The stairs were tricky. One step, one foot, the other foot, another step. But sometimes he'd just grab at his trousers, pull his leg up and walk right up or right down. I could tell by the sound of his steps when he was tired. Step, clump, step, clump. Mostly that was when he was having asthma. When he was having an attack breathing and walking at the same time was very hard.

 I remember the gun as clearly as I do his leg. It was blue-black metal with wood on the handle. He let me hold it and I was always surprised at how heavy it was for such a small thing. It had a certain smell. Metallic, oily. Serious and scary. One night my father and mother were asleep in their bed when he heard a noise. Somebody coming down the hall, quietly, sneaking along the carpeted floor. He reached under his pillow and took hold of the gun, raised it toward the dim light at the door to the bedroom, watched as a tall man in black approached the door.

"Stop where you are. I have a gun," he called out.

"For Christ's sake, Jimmy, it's me. Carrol. Put that damned thing down before you kill somebody."

It was my father's nephew, Carrol. He was my father's age and they were best friends. Carrol had been in Hartford at a late party and had decided to spend the night with us instead of driving home. They laughed about it at breakfast the next day, but I didn't think it was funny. I loved Carrol and I loved my father. What had almost happened was too awful to think about. Still, I would go into my parent's bedroom and feel around under my father's pillow, wrap my hand around the butt of the pistol and pull it out into daylight. I would put my nose up to the barrel and smell the oil. I would heft the gun in my small hand. The feeling of being in charge of so much danger was powerful. I could scare the things that lived under my bed and in my closet. I could kill the kidnappers and robbers that waited for night to climb up ladders and into the bedrooms of little girls. I would slide the gun back under my father's pillow and walk away feeling invincible. The feeling didn't last but it was heady for the moment. My father never knew what I did. He had told my brother and me not to touch the gun when he wasn't there and he trusted us to do what he said. His nearly killing Carrol made me careful for many months, but in the end I went back to sneaking in and hefting the gun whenever I felt powerless or lonely or just curious to see if it still felt the same. It did. For years I equated having a gun with making up for things one lacked, a leg or size enough to matter or power enough to prevail.

There were other guns. A rifle, long and thin with a polished wood stock. And two shot guns. My father had one and then he bought another. He gave it to my mother for her birthday so she could go deer hunting with him. She said thank you and went. I never touched those guns. My father had a skeet gun at our cabin. He and his friends would spend all day standing on the deck, calling out to whoever was taking his turn at working the skeet gun.

"Pull!" BANG "Nice one, Jimmy." "Pull!" BANG "How the hell could you miss with that elephant gun a yours, Charlie?"

It was a noisy way to spend a Sunday, but they never seemed to get tired of it. "Nothing like shootin' skeet." One or another of my father's friends would say, "Hey, Shirley, want to try?" and hold out a shotgun to me at nine or ten. I'd say "No, thanks" and go into the cabin, find a book, and read, listening all the while to the crack of the guns and the hollering of the men.

And then there were the deer. The two years of the men killing deer were what finally cured me of wanting to hold my father's guns. Whenever my brother and I went into the shed at the top of the rise behind the cabin there would be a deer carcass hanging from a huge hook in the ceiling. Sometimes it was so fresh that our father had not had time to skin it. Other times it would be bloody meat, the hooves of the deer cut off, the head cut off, just the raw flesh of the body hanging there. "Curing", my father called it. Nothing was ever going to *cure* those deer. They were the deadest things I'd ever seen. My father would sit on the porch cleaning his shot gun or his rifle, smiling and humming or whistling. Happy as he ever was. Relaxed and satisfied as he ever was. My mother would cook the venison, stew it over night on the wood stove and serve it for lunch the next day. She was a good cook and everybody said how much they enjoyed the stew. It tasted like blood to me.

INCIDENT IN WOODS

known man
familiar
he walks before her into woods
beckoning
becomes sun-dappled satyr
as he goes

sheltered by oak and fir
he turns his stallion eyes on her
and reaches out
she is surprised
gentled by his hairy hand
    upon her flesh
his hooves disturb the leaves
make a nest beneath her
his breath in her mouth is wild
and tastes of hay

he mounts
and she receives

when he is known again
man form
familiar
they curl together in the leaves
    and sleep
in bird watched darkness until dawn

OLD WOMEN

    old women wear their gray hair long
    to their shoulders, down the back
    when we're not looking
    they take out the pins and let it loose
    they wash it at the pump in cold water
    rinse it with vinegar or lemon to cut the soap
    dry it in the sun on an old blue turkish towel
    they comb it out and leave it down upon their shoulders
    when we're not there

    old women go shoeless
    walk in the grass at dawn
    feel crisp green dampness
    between their toes
    after rain they splash in shallow puddles
    hold faded denim skirts high, gypsy fashion
    and skip a bit
    to feel the mud

old women laugh out loud
low raucous sounds
when we're not around
they giggle at nothing
and cry at everything
when we're not home
they lie on thin gray blankets
sobbing into feather pillows all night long
old women kiss old men or one another
with open mouths
they shed their flannel night clothes
go to bed together
for comfort
and for all the other reasons
old women wear their hair down long
and walk barefoot
when we're not there

NOVEMBER HEAT WAVE

these basking days of autumn
    have caused a crisis in the growing cycle
    in my back yard
the yellow maple leaves fall in confusion
    forced from the branch
    as tender buds begin to form
    six months too soon
global warming
indian summer
my addle-pated red geraniums don't care
they bloom and bloom and bloom
pretending, I think, to be poinsettias

SHOPPING LIST

the cave mother
puts a charred stick
in her cave daughter's hand
helps her trace
the clear outline
of a deer
on the firelit wall
she rouses the cave father
points and says
bring us one of those for supper

THE USUAL

when we were together we always ate Chinese
meeting by accident in an Italian restaurant
a long time after
each in the casual company of others
we brush lips hello
and pass through one another
our invisible atoms
passionate with recognition
we fuse in the familiar
and step apart
each carrying ions of the other
we return to unsuspecting tables
I order tortellini and a salad of arugula
your back is to me
I can't hear what you order
when we were together
it would have been fried wonton
and lobster cantonese

SAFE

tented in attic eaves and rafters
illicit candle
and a book
alone in moted air
beyond the reach
above the sound

pulse of old blood
urges me to bed at the top of the tree
safe from tigers

ORRIE

A Story

"Stop pushing. I'm up."

Orrie Campbell awoke to a gray dawn alone in her narrow bed. There was no shade to draw at her window nor any curtain. She liked it that way. Her mother, the same mother who had named her Oracle after the Vaudeville Theater in the home town she so quietly and desperately yearned for, had offered both or either.

"I'll get you a shade at Kresge's next time we go in town. Or I can make you some curtains outta that remnant I got at the White Elephant. It's got birds and trees on it like you like."

But Orrie declined. She loved to see the stars and the moon as she fell asleep. She wanted the dawn to wake her. She thrilled to the lightning that came with the wind and rain storms of summer. What she really wanted was to have a tree house where she could sleep every night, even in the snow. This attic room was as close as she could come to the top of the maple tree outside her window. She was pleased that her mother let her settle her few things up here away from the rest of the house.

"Don't push me. I won't listen if you push."

Orrie reached down beside the bed to where her underwear was lying on the floor. There was no chair in the room and only a set of shelves to act as a bureau. She left her underpants on the floor each night so she would not have to get out of bed to put them on.

"Oatmeal's getting cold, Orrie."

Her mother's voice came up the attic stairs from the kitchen two floors below, losing volume as it traveled. Another reason for Orrie to cherish her aerie. She pulled on the shorts she had worn the day before and buttoned a clean yellow cotton shirt around her thin chest. No shoes. It was summer and she would be free to go barefoot until school in September. The bottoms of her feet were callused and no amount of scrubbing with yellow soap would get them really clean. Orrie ran a mostly toothless comb through her short brown hair and started down the stairs. No mirror to check that what she had done would meet with her mother's approval.

"Go away. I'm not listening," she said aloud to what was nagging at her, urging her.

She was careful not to speak of what she thought of as her *messages* to her parents. Or to anyone. She knew she was called fey and odd and sometimes, by her grandmother, moon child. She had no wish to add to the catalogue of strangeness the adults around her were collecting. The list was already longer than she knew.

She kept her pet garter snake in a shoe box in the garden shed. When she went to school she wore the snake around her neck, under her blouse or sweater, where it stayed, she thought, because it enjoyed her body warmth. The boys she knew teased the girls with bits of rope or string thrown at them suddenly in the school yard. "Girls are scared green of snakes," they'd yell. She showed her snake to her friend Ted one recess. He must have told the others because, while they did not avoid her, neither did they tease her.

She calmed the small bands of feral dogs that came into their yard every month or so year round, yapping and snarling and snatching at the hands of anyone who came near, anyone but Orrie. She would croon what her father called her gibberish at the mongrels and they would lope out of the yard and down the road, as peaceful as a herd of cows.

She warned of thunderstorms and wind and hail while the sky was bright with sun and the leaves hung limp on the trees. She found things, lost articles, for her family and for anyone who asked. Her fingers felt the object, a pair of glasses, a key, a Boy Scout pin, before they closed around it. People used her gifts but they called her odd. She would not talk about the thing that spoke to her.

"Your Daddy's gone to work," her mother said as Orrie came into the kitchen. "I let you sleep in. Looks like a real hot day. We won't try to get too much done beyond the washing. Should dry in an hour. Eat your breakfast then you can help me set up the wash tub."

Orrie didn't have to say much when she was with her mother. Her mother carried on whole conversations as if Orrie were answering, commenting, agreeing. She did the same thing with Orrie's father. Once in a while, when he had a nickel or a dime left at the end of the week he would buy a cigar and, right in the middle of a harange, walk out into the back yard to smoke. She never seemed to notice he was gone. He would give the gold colored paper band from around the cigar to Orrie. "A gold ring for my best girl." She didn't put the paper band on her finger but placed each one in the cigar box her father had given her when she was six. The inside of the box smelled like him, like his breath when he kissed her good night. The cigar bands were a talisman. A thing she would have if anything ever happened to her father. It did not occur to her to keep a charm against her mother's possible disappearance. Her mother was rooted, like the tree outside her attic window. Winds might blow and rain might pound but the tree endured. Her mother was eternal and needed no protection.

"Grab that other handle, Orrie. Help me get this thing up on the bench."

Orrie and her mother lifted the galvanized wash tub from its place on the back porch and carried it down the back steps to the bench set in the yard. The hose connection, a stand pipe with a spigot on top, was just to the left of the bottom step. Handy for cold water but the kettles of hot water it took to fill the tub had to be carried from the coal stove in the kitchen, across the porch, down the steps, then to be poured into the tub. Orrie was old enough at ten to be trusted with transporting the steaming tea kettle and the soup pot. Her mother would help her with the huge canning kettle, one of them on each side holding on to the wire bale with dish towels clasped in their hands, hot vapor bathing their arms and faces and curling her mother's hair around her face. Orrie brought the dirty clothes and bed linens down from the second floor, then made a second trip to gather her own few things and the bottom sheet from her bed. She slept with a light quilt over her in summer and with a woolen blanket and a heavier quilt in winter. She resisted her mother's attempt to put a top sheet on her bed. "I wake up with it tangled all around my legs, Mommy." Her mother talked through her explanation and the top sheet was forgotten.

Once her mother had begun soaking and scrubbing and rinsing and hanging the laundry Orrie was free. After breakfast she had buttered a slice of bread, added a generous sprinkling of brown sugar, doubled the bread over on itself and wrapped the sandwich in a piece of waxed paper. It bulged now from the back pocket of her shorts and would be her lunch when she felt hungry. Orrie was required to be present at breakfast and at dinner, but barring any special chores, the time between was hers.

Giving in now to the urgency of her internal message she said, "I'm going to walk to the store, Mama. Do you need anything?"

Her mother, bent over the wash tub, round muscled arms moving like pistons as she rubbed a pair of her husband's long pants over the corrugated surface of the washboard, did not look up from her work. "There's a dime in the cookie jar. Get a loaf of bread. Not that pasty stuff. Get whole wheat. Your Daddy likes whole wheat. And mind you don't go the river way. That river's unpredictable."

Orrie had run up the stairs and into the kitchen as soon as she heard "Get a loaf of bread." The rest of what her mother had to say she knew by heart. She knew her father liked whole wheat bread and she knew she wouldn't go the river way. She might return that way but her mother never mentioned the return trip. She also knew that the bread was nine cents and that she could spend the penny change on candy or gum or a pickle from the big barrel beside the counter.

"I hear you," she said aloud as she left the front yard and started along the dirt road that led to the country store a mile and a half away and, if you kept going for another eight miles, to the small town with the gas pumps and the Post Office. She scuffled her bare feet as she walked so the dry dirt, soft as talc, sifted through her toes.

Afternoon was the critical time. No specific hour, but Orrie had had a clear vision of the scene when the urgings had begun that morning. She had felt the sun beginning to lose its noon heat, had seen the field where it would happen, had felt the humid air of late summer on her face. She knew she had to deliver the message before the lunch break.

"I'll be in plenty of time. They don't have lunch on the farm till one. Lots of time."

Orrie passed the landscape she had always known: low shrub at the roadside, weeds and sumac giving way to scrub trees and, following the river bank half a mile back from the road, aspen and bright patches of birch. This farm land had been formed by the river which flooded often enough to make rich top soil and to send the few families who lived in the valley to the second stories of their houses to await the reappearance of dry land. There were no houses between hers and Ferry's General Store and Feed Merchants. No automobile would pass, scarce as they were in this time and place. Occasionally a horse drawn hay wagon or a tractor would approach in a cloud of dust, the driver waving to her, familiar as the landscape, whoever he was. One day Orrie would tell her grandchildren "There were no sidewalks when I was a girl." They would be unable to imagine such a thing.

The hazy August sun made heat wave mirages in the dust ahead of Orrie. She thought of the vast deserts of sand she had seen in pictures in the geography book on the teacher's desk at school. The paragraph under the pictures had described sand storms and mirages with words like 'chimera' and 'phantasm' that made Orrie long to experience the mind teasing mirages.

"These here on my road must be babies. Think what a real mirage might be."

Concentrating on the shimmering images before her kept her from hearing the urging inside. This feeling of a time limit was new. Still, she did not hurry until the faded wood building that was the store came into view. Then she stopped scuffling and began to walk quickly, with purpose, sweat running down her face and into the collar of her blouse. She stepped onto the small porch with its leaning overhang of a roof and pushed the torn screen door open. It closed behind her with a thump. The inside of the store was shadowed and cool. Mrs. Ferry, the lean, smiling woman who, with her tall angry husband owned the store, stood behind the counter talking with Mrs. Kulas from the farm across the road.

"Try rubbing your knee with vinegar. Vinegar's good for rheumatism. You can put a poultice on at night. You know, soak a rag in hot vinegar and tie it around your knee," Mrs. Ferry was saying in a low, private voice to the enormous Mrs. Kulas, her legs bulging over the tops of her lisle stockings, rolled below her knees, just below the hem of her flowered cotton dress.

"Nobody knows the misery. Hurts all day and no sleep at night,' Mrs. Kulas answered.

'Like my mother,' Orrie thinks, standing back from the counter, waiting her turn. 'Didn't hear a word.'

"What can I get for you, Miss Orrie Campbell?"

Mrs. Ferry's voice was louder now and teasing. She always gave Orrie her full title and was the first and only person to call her 'Miss'. Teasing or not, Orrie loved it.

"A loaf of whole wheat bread for my mother, please, Mrs. Ferry. And a licorice whip for me, please."

Orrie slid the dime, warm from her hand, across the wooden counter toward Mrs. Ferry. She took the brown paper bag holding the bread and her candy from Mrs. Ferry's fingers, took a deep breath and said, "How's Will, Mrs. Ferry?"

"He's right as rain, Miss Orrie. Thanks for asking. He's helping his father clear the farm of corn shucks this morning. I'll give him your hello at supper."

"Mrs. Ferry, I have to say something more. Please don't let Will work the field this afternoon."

Orrie's heart was pounding so hard she could feel it against her blouse.

"What's that? Why, honey?"

Mrs. Ferry glanced at Mrs. Kulas who had settled her huge behind on the barrel of grain in a corner of the store and looked planted for the day. The look the two women exchanged said 'Queer one, this'.

"Something bad's going to happen. Something to do with machinery. Will should stay away from machinery till tomorrow. You will tell him when you take him his lunch, won't you, Mrs. Ferry?"

"Sure will. Say hello to your mother and father for Mr. Ferry and me."

Orrie was out the door, off the porch and walking through the undergrowth beside the store on her way to the river bank when Mrs. Ferry said to Mrs. Kulas, "She's sweet, that Orrie, but her head's off somewhere in the clouds. Got a crush on Will. Big good lookin' boy, if I say it myself."

What she said when she handed Will his lunch packet at the edge of the field where he was working with the corn stalk baler was, "Your little girl friend Orrie says hello."

Orrie made her way through the low brush to the river bank. Her thoughts were quiet now that she had delivered her message. Mrs. Ferry would act to save her son and all would be well. She walked toward home for ten minutes, keeping her eyes on the slowly moving water, looking for frogs or fish or water spiders. At the bend where the river narrowed, a tree had fallen half way across the water. She sat on the natural bridge, trailing her sandy feet in the cold water, and let her mind wander. Nothing came to her, nothing warned her.

When she reached home Orrie sat on the wide front steps of her house to eat her sandwich. She drew a hop scotch grid in the dirt driveway beside the house and played by herself until the sun made long shadows across the lawn. At twilight she climbed the stairs and went through the quiet house to the kitchen where she found her mother ashen faced, holding the receiver of the wall mounted telephone in her right hand.

"That was Mrs. Kulas on the party line. Will Ferry had his left arm taken off by the baler. Almost bled to death before they could get help. My stars, what a horror. That nice boy crippled for life. Be no use on the farm now what with one arm and all. They're taking him in to the hospital now. Probably have to have a transfusion."

Orrie stopped hearing her mother's voice and heard only the scream Will must have screamed as his arm was ripped from his body. She had done what she could and it was not enough. Should she have run to the store when she woke that morning with the message strong in her mind, the urging pushing her to act? She had instead eaten breakfast, helped her mother, taken her time walking the road to Ferry's.

She began doing penance. She took the shoe box to the far end of the back yard where the lilac bush and the tomato plants made a narrow shade on the otherwise sun crisped lawn and there she let her garter snake slither free. He was gone from her sight before she had the lid back on the box. She buried the cigar box that smelled of her father, buried all but one of the golden paper rings that kept her father safe. That one paper band she tucked above the rafter over her bed. She decided that her father should not be placed in peril for her mistake. One band would do as well to protect him as the nineteen she had buried.

Orrie knew now that she was not the proper one to receive her messages. She was weak and stubborn and slow. She would find a way to keep the urgings quiet. She discovered that if she was reading, really reading, absorbing what she read, she could block out the messages. There was only one book in the house, an almanac from 1912, filled with facts and figures and charts and maps that kept her attention for long hours. She read it through more times than she counted. When school opened again, she began to spend the time between her last class and the arrival of the school bus at the library, the small brick building next to the school. She was old enough to take books out, to carry them home with her on the school bus, but what she loved to do was to lose herself in a book in the quiet of the reading room. On more than one autumn afternoon she missed the bus and walked the two and a half miles home, library book under her arm.

The hardest part of her penance was going to the store for her mother. Mrs. Ferry no longer called her 'Miss'. She was now Oracle May Campbell said in a way that made Orrie think it was a curse. She didn't blame Mrs. Ferry for being angry with her, but she knew that the woman bore part of the responsibility. She had not warned her son, had not taken Orrie seriously.

Will appeared at school with his shirt sleeve hanging empty, his books strapped together and flung over his shoulder, the strap held in his right hand. He smiled at Orrie when they happened to meet but they had never had a speaking acquaintance so Orrie was satisfied that he held no grudge. Perhaps he didn't know of her part in his loss. The summer after the accident he learned to drive the tractor with one hand, he swam at the quarry, and he danced with Mary Craven at the church socials.

Orrie watched Will heal and began to feel a healing of her own. She allowed herself to receive the messages again. She found a silver dollar in a barrel of flour for one of her mother's friends from church. She told Harry Selden that she saw fire in his horse barn. He removed a lantern that had been close to the horses' stall and there was no fire. Harry Selden thanked her right in front of her mother and father.

"Remarkable young lady, your daughter. Would have been a real tragedy to lose those horses."

People still called her odd and fantastical, but she no longer minded. She began to take their words as setting her apart in a way that made her happy. She read now for the pleasure of it and she let the urgings in whenever they came.

It was not until she was grown, had married, moved away and come back to show her first child to her mother and father, that she and Mrs. Ferry exchanged words that had no sting in them. Orrie opened the still broken screen door and approached the counter, her infant daughter in her arms.

Mrs. Ferry, thinner, sitting now behind the counter, no longer able to stand for the long hours the store was open, looked up and said, "Miss Orrie Campbell, is that your own child in your arms?"

"It is, Mrs. Ferry. I wanted her to meet you so when she's old enough to come in for her licorice whip you'll know each other."

"She's the spit of you, Orrie."

Orrie shifted the baby in her arms, folded back a corner of the swaddled blanket and bent to touch her lips to the top of her daughter's head.

"She's very like me, far as we can tell."

BASKET FOR EDITH

I have woven a basket for you
working from the center out
radiants and reeds I have plaited
bending and binding
resistant grasses
beyond the curve of nature
and cast a spell to keep the handle on

for a day and a night
it sat on the sea-ward window sill
to dry
and to absorb sea sounds
I have filled it with moss
sea lavender and shells
and the ghost claws of tiny crabs
    papery and barely pink

I have woven a basket for you
    to place beside your bed
it carries dreams
that only you can dream

AT THE 'Y' WITH EDITH

weightless as in dreams
warm supported comforted
in a pool so large
so deep
it may be tidal
we jelly-fish about
not swimming
yet not sinking

suspended in amniotic limbo
we are unavailable for comment

FROM THE WINDOW OF THE METROLINER

NEW YORK TO WASHINGTON, D. C.

1

In Baltimore
The rows of houses wear their Hopper fronts
This one barn red
    this gray
        this white
No Hopper light though
On this rain threatened February afternoon

2

The station master wears his hat
    patent leather visor at a careful angle
Long blue coat hanging open
    he stands with his hands in his pockets
        unfocussed eyes cast down
Seeing some phantom time table
    in the wet bricks shine of the station platform

3

I am at the southern reaches of the Delaware
    in another time
My companion is not you
The river is the one upon whose banks we walked
    in another place
I cannot turn from the window and say
Remember

4

In Delaware
A field of crows lifts off
Banks into the gray sky
Skims ocher stubble
And flies off to Arles

5

Crossing a railroad bridge
    I look out over water
To the expected seam of sky and river
    and find a watercolor blur of fog
I am floating
Horizonless
In a train which clings to the rails
    to keep from falling off the earth

THE ICE HOUSE

Memoir

"Did you hear that?"

My mother's head swings from right to left. Where is the sound coming from? We hear nothing but the normal sounds of the nursing floor. A muted telephone, a food cart whooshing by on rubber wheels. Her tone is insistent. Those are not the sounds she means.

"Oh, I know. It's the cow over there in the corner," she says, indicating with a sweep of her graceful hand a far corner of the room she shares with Ruth, the bed bound woman who has been a beauty and who now sleeps most of the time. "I hear it all the time, munching, munching," her eyes wide with emphasis.

"What's it eating, Mom?" I join her in her hallucination.

She scowls at me, pulls her lips down in scorn. How can I be so dense, so forgetful of what cows eat?

"Corn cobs, of course."

Of course. The virtual world in which she lives following her heart attack and the consequent deprivation of oxygen to her brain has many of the same rules, the same logic, as the real world in which my husband and I sit, he on the edge of the bed, I on my mother's closed commode. She sits, fully dressed, in her lounge chair, looking eagerly toward the door into the hall. Waiting for visitors, I think. We are not enough, my husband and I. She looks at me when I speak to her, but it's hard to tell if she knows who I am. That is, she knows I'm her daughter, but I haven't had a name since 'the shock', as she refers to it. "I had this shock but I'm better now. My bags are packed and I'm ready to go !"

The Hospice aide, Sherrill, helped my mother dress this morning, sat with her through breakfast encouraging her to have 'just a little bite of the toast, Elberta'. Then she tidied the few square feet of my mother's room here in the Masonic Home. She put the used Kleenex and paper cups in the waste basket, dirty mugs on the tray in the hall, smoothed the bed clothes and plumped the pillows. I know she did all this and more because it was done when we arrived and my mother will never do it again. Until now my mother has kept house as if this tiny space that holds a bed, a bedside table, a bureau, a hospital table and a commode, were any one of the many homes we have shared with her over seventy years, my brother and I. And she did it as happily and with as little complaint as she ever did. Her person, too, has been immaculate and her clothes, clean and colorful and becoming. Until now she has gotten up every morning, washed at the shared sink on the far wall, applied her blush and powder and lipstick at the mirror above that sink, chosen an 'outfit' for the day and has dressed with care and pleasure. "The others look to me to be properly dressed. I get a lot of compliments on this blue blouse."

Today Sherrill has brushed my mother's curly white hair into a halo and has dressed her in a short-sleeved floral blouse and blue polyester slacks. It's hot here on the skilled nursing floor. The rooms were redecorated last year and are fresh and bright, but there was no attempt to add air-conditioning to this part of the building. A huge wall-mounted fan pushes hot air from my mother's side of the room to Ruth's side. I wonder if it would be better just to turn it off, but I don't do it. Mother used to say that just having the fan blades turning made her feel cooler.

"Get me a shirt," my mother says, tugging at the front of her blouse. I see that the buttons down the front gap and show her bra. She's on a quick visit back to reality.

I go to her clothes rack, a short double rack pushed into the wall closet just inside the door to the hall. She and Ruth share this closet, but the bureaus are each their own. I take a round necked cotton pull-over from the rack and hold it up.

"How's this one?" I ask.

She is grabbing her shirt with her left hand, trying to pull it down over her right shoulder. The oxygen tube she wears is tangled and has been yanked from her nose.

"Wait a minute, Mom. I have to get one that opens down the front. I forgot about your oxygen."

She doesn't hear me. She keeps at her task, shrugging her shoulder out of the still buttoned neck of the blouse. I grab a flowered shirt, a near twin to the one she's wearing, and hurry over to her. She subsides and lets me remove the offending blouse. She cooperates with my efforts to put its replacement on without further disturbing the thin plastic hose that is now her principle life line.

"Let me help you put your tube back in your nose, Mom."

"I'll leave it off. I don't need it."

I replace the tube and she doesn't seem to notice.

It is natural to me to be ministering to my mother. Not physically until now, but emotionally. It was clear to me when I was twelve and my father died that I should do what he would have done. It does her an injustice for me to leave it at that. It's only part of what happened. She found a job within three months of my father's death, a death that left her without insurance, without savings. In fact she plunged into the next decade of raising my brother and me without a thought to her own needs, her own comfort. I would not understand that she was deeply depressed during this time until I myself hit a patch of postpartum disconnect that lasted nearly two years. Her removal from and simultaneous dependence on me was no longer a mystery. After all, I had felt pretty much the same way about my own tiny son and daughter during my time of depression. Meanwhile, I was and am friend, mother, helpmate to my mother. Always I have failed to satisfy her just enough to keep either of us from being really happy. Now, in my seventy second year, in her ninety third, I seem to be doing things right, or at least, better. It won't last.

"I went to the ice house yesterday. I like going there. The people are all contented and happy. They don't want to be disturbed."

She is smiling and her eyes are clear. She sees the ice house and it makes her happy.

"Can you go there whenever you want or do you have to be asked?" I say.

She thinks hard, her forehead deeply furrowed, her right hand fluttering at her lips.

"No, I can't go whenever I want to. That would be nice, though. I'll work on it."

I pull back the curtain between my mother's bed and her room-mate's and see that Ruth's bed is empty. A small, gray woman is sitting on a straight chair near the door. She speaks to the volunteer who has come to take my mother's all but untouched lunch tray. She who ordered and devoured the seafood special when we took her to lunch just short weeks ago has forgotten what food is for.

"May I rest on the bed?" this wisp of a woman asks. Like a four-year-old well-mannered little girl asking if she may have a cookie, I think. My mother's generation, timid and unsure about what's hers, what she may share in.

The volunteer says, "Of course you may. This is your home." She puts down mother's tray, helps the tiny woman onto the bed, covers her with an afghan, picks up the tray and leaves, smiling back at all of us. "You two ladies have a nice afternoon."

So Ruth is no longer here.

"What happened to Ruth, Mom?" I ask. What do I suppose happened?

"Do you mean 'where is she?'"

"Yes."

"That's between her and God," my mother says. I have been put in my place. What business is it of mine where Ruth has gone?

When we leave my mother turns petulant.

"I don't want to be left here all alone. You can't go now. You stay and keep me company."

Not that I don't understand how she feels. Loneliness looms larger than death for the moment. She isn't even asking that her daughter stay. She doesn't care who it is in the chair by her bed. Just don't leave her to do this thing alone. It's the whining that strikes me as new. It's true that she has always had trouble asking for what she needs, but she has never, ever whined before. I kiss her thin, dry lips (the oxygen tube is sucking the life fluids out of her) and I say the obvious words of reassurance, the words that wouldn't fool the Beanie Baby frog she clutches to her breast. "There are all kinds of people here, Mom, and they'll all look after you. You won't be alone for a minute."

She stares at me, seeing me for the fool I am, and then turns her head away. She has never deliberately turned from me before. I know she won't remember ten minutes from now that I have been here at all, but I want to stay. I want to sit by her and hold her hand and reminisce. She holds my history and it's all slipping away. I'm the one who wants to say "Don't go".

Last Friday, just a week and two days ago, she had a heart attack. That's what the doctor is calling it. "We'll say it was a heart attack. She had severe fibrillation and was unable to breath for about three hours. We provided oxygen and morphine as per her and your instructions." DNR. Do not resuscitate. Mother had filled out the forms when she came to live at The Masonic Home four years ago. One must execute a living will, leave written instructions for one's burial or cremation, give someone, preferably a near relative, power of attorney, before entering the Home. She had done all of that and it was no surprise to my brother or me that she did not want a respirator nor any heroic measures. We have always talked about such things openly and without sentimentality. Mother had been having some fibrillation off and on for two weeks, enough so she had been moved from her room on the Skilled Nursing Floor to the Acute Care Unit. That's where she was when she had her heart attack. Just that morning when the doctor asked if she was clear on what she wanted in the event of a severe occurrence she had said, "I'm ninety-three years old. Will you stop bothering me." The doctor laughed when he phoned to tell me of their exchange, to settle in his own mind that what she wanted was what the family wanted. "She's so wonderfully sure. She certainly calls a spade a spade."

I telephoned her every evening at five and that evening she had said, "He's just reassuring himself. I wrote all that down four years ago. I've done that work. I don't want any tubes. Don't let anybody break my ribs or crush my chest, either. I want them to leave me alone."

Her tone was serious but she ended with a laugh. The laugh means, I don't want to be a bother. Don't go to any trouble for me. See how undemanding I am. The unspoken is always: *Make things right for me. Go first so I don't trip over anything. Carry my bundles.*

"I'll see to it, Mom. You just relax. Don't worry about any of that stuff. Nobody's going to bother you," I said, wondering how I could prevent it. "My dear, good friend," she said and we hung up.

At 4:17 AM the phone beside my bed rang. Once. I had it in my hand and was wide awake.

"Hello?"

"Hello, is this Shirley Homes? This is Masonic calling."

The woman's voice was clear, quiet and authoritative.
"Yes, this is she," I answered, trying to sound as if it were mid-day, as if I had been expecting her call.
"Your mother, Bert Snow, has had a very bad night. Her breathing has been extremely labored and she is now in a state of near exhaustion. We have stabilized her breathing with medication and oxygen."
"Should I come?"
"Yes."
Not "morning will be enough time" but "Yes".
And then she said, "Drive very carefully," and hung up. Those words, her caring for me, not just for my mother, were the words that brought the tears. Quick and over in a minute. Get my husband up, get dressed, get to Mom, my thoughts, clear and orderly, not letting feeling in again. I changed my mind three times on what to wear. The black suit too funereal, the jeans too casual, the linen pants suit cool and comfortable in case I don't get to change again for a while. I didn't take a shower and I hated that. My mother has always been the cleanest little person. How could I come to her bedside less than freshly scrubbed, but my anxiety wouldn't permit the ten minutes the shower and drying my hair would take.

We drove along the winding curves of the Merritt Parkway in the fog of predawn, Herb sitting forward over the wheel, concentrating on getting us there alive. At nearly seventy-three his night vision is marginal and we try to avoid traveling after dark. We were silent during the drive. Nothing to say. My mother would either be alive when we arrived or she wouldn't. We would either be seeing to the final things or we wouldn't. There was no way to prepare for either eventuality. Just sit quietly in my seat and try not to bother Herb. Because of the fog, the ride which normally takes an hour and a quarter, took just over two hours. Herb pulled off the parkway at Exit 65, made the left that swings around into the parking lot in front of the Home and we got out of the car. Herb's face was white with fatigue and I knew I probably looked the same, washed out and old. It was beginning to get light as we walked up the long sloped sidewalk that leads to the awning covered entrance of the familiar building. My legs were stiff and my mouth tasted of metal as we went through the automatic glass door into the lobby. A woman emptying a waste basket looked up and smiled. "Good morning. Terrible fog," she said

"Everybody speaks to you in this place. It's nice," Herb said, heading off to the right toward the Cafe, toward the rest rooms.

"You go," I said following him along the carpeted corridor, its walls lined with cheerful water colors and with pictures of Wallingford and the Home through the years. "I'm going right up. It's on the third floor."

Herb came with me in the elevator, keeping me company. Staying close, maybe for his own comfort, too. "There'll be a john up there," he said.

A nurse was getting on the elevator as we got off. She stepped back into the hall and asked if we needed help.

"We're looking for my mother. She's in the ACU," I said.

"Follow me," she said and she was off down the hall, down another hall, a turn and another turn and we were there.

"Thank you," I said. "I'd never have found it on my own."

She wished us well and hurried off.

Then we were in my mother's room. I thought at first that the woman in the first bed was Mom. A friend of ours had told of going to visit his very sick mother in the hospital and of having sat for many minutes comforting a woman on a stretcher before realizing that she wasn't his mother. He said he had felt foolish and so did I. Herb had gone directly to my mother's bed, the bed by the window. She has the bed by the window in her own room, too. The view is essential to her happiness.

I came around the end of the bed and moved up to where she lay. She was inert. I was sure we were too late.

Her face was the gray that means there is no blood flowing anywhere in the body. I'd seen it before. My father's face on the white pillow when I was twelve. My young aunt seven years later asking for macaroni and cheese, eating two mouthsful from the spoon I held to her lips with what seemed to me like pleasure and then dying less than an hour later, her face the same drawn gray-white as my mother's was at that moment.

I sat in the leather armchair beside her bed and groped under the thin blanket and the sheet for her hand.

"She's warm," I said to Herb.

Warm but unresponsive.

A nurse came in and uncovered her thin, white feet, feet she was proud of. "Not a callus or a corn anywhere. The feet of a young girl," she would say, holding them out in front of her and wiggling her toes. The nurse ran her finger along the sole of Mom's foot. Nothing. Her toes did not respond. The nurse covered her feet again and smiled at me.

"She had a rough night, but I think she's a little better. Quieter, anyway," she said and turned to see to the woman in the other bed.

She's better? Better than what? I could only hold her hand, stroke her fragile skin and wait. Were we waiting for her to die, Herb and I, sitting without speaking in this large, comfortable room where the oxygen tube that Mom was breathing through came out of the wall like a mechanical umbilicus and where all of the other machines, the ones my mother has refused to consider, sat waiting to be put to use? The doctor's medical assistant came in and said that she was the one who had called me. She apologized for waking me but not for getting us here.

"We can't tell much right now. The morphine is making her comfortable, but her arteries are very blocked. We'll just have to wait and see what happens."

She left and we sat for the next two hours watching my mother breath. She did not respond to her name or to being touched in all that time.

"I think she's frowning," I said at about nine thirty. "I hope she's not uncomfortable. I think I'll get a nurse."

I went to the nurse's station and said to the pretty young woman, standing behind the counter, holding a phone to her ear, "My mother looks like she might be feeling pain. Can you give her more morphine?"

The nurse put the phone down, picked up a packet and led the way to Mom's bedside. She inserted a needle into the shunt on my mother's wrist and pressed evenly on the plunger.

"We don't have her on a drip. No tubes," she said.

"I know. Thank you," I said.

On an impulse I picked up the large stuffed green frog that had become my mother's comfort since her great-granddaughter, our granddaughter, Ali, had given it to her for her ninety-third birthday. "I want something soft to cuddle," she had said. "Something that will hang over my arm and won't look like anything real. I don't want people to think that I think I have a live pet." Smoochie, a Beanie Buddy, whom Mom rechristened Freddie became her instant friend and confidant. He lay on her bed close to her right hand, but I knew she wouldn't be hugging him.

"Mom, look who's here. Freddie," I said and waggled him in front of her.

Her eyes popped open and she laughed out loud. A real laugh.

"I wondered where he was," she said, the words only slightly slurred.

My brother and his wife, their two daughters, their son-in-law and one of their grandchildren arrived. Expecting to find, as we had, a dying woman. They came to say good-by. My mother had other ideas. Her room was filled with people and, whether she knew who we were or not, it was time for laughter. Party time. The nurse pushed the button that raised the head of her bed and she sat up, enthroned one might have thought. She squealed with delight, pointing at each one, laughing at whatever was said.

"I don't know what's going on," she said. "I really can't fathom it, but I see I'm entertaining."

She was, too. She was funny and sweet and insightful. Hyper, her eyes rolling to emphasize her words, her hands waving and pointing. She was "on" and we all loved her performance. Friends from Simsbury where she had lived for a number of years came to pay their respects and stayed to laugh with her and to wonder at her resilience and at her humor.

"You," she said, pointing at her granddaughter's husband, "Go home and play with your children. Not games with rules. You make up the rules. You like to win."

Bingo.

"You keep him," she said to me, flicking her finger in the direction of my husband. "You keep him. He's a good one."

Bingo, again.

Two nights later. I am on the phone with my mother. A nurse has had to hand her the receiver.

"Hi, Mom. How are you? This is Shirley," I say.

"I know that. I know my own daughter, for heaven's sake."

Oh, good, her voice is not thready though I can hear the rasp from the oxygen.

"What you been up to today?" I ask.

"I took a couple of trips," she says. To X-ray? To the bathroom? Where can this survivor of so recent a heart attack have gone?

"I went to Texas and then I went over to Arizona. I took the train. I rode in the baggage car."

"That sounds wonderful, Mom. A really full day. Are you tired?"

"Yes, a little. Hard to breath sometimes."

"Why did you go by baggage car?"

"It doesn't cost anything and they tell you when to get off. There were other people traveling that way. The only thing I didn't like was that I had the wrong clothes with me."

"You should have bought some new things while you were out there," I say.

She laughs, the full throated laugh I've heard for all of my seventy-two years.

"Well, I guess I should have. After all, the *trip* didn't cost me anything."

I laugh, too. Most of our daily phone conversations over the years have ended with laughter.

My brother and I agree that our mother should be returned to her own room as soon as possible. We have initiated Hospice Care and have been assured that Hospice can give her the same treatment she would receive in the Acute Care Unit. We both want her to be in familiar surroundings.

When a woman from Social Services calls a few days after Mother has come back to her room, she asks, "How would you feel about changing your mother to a room across the hall, closer to the nurse's station?"

I'm angry. "I wouldn't respond positively at all. What's the problem?"

"Oh, don't worry. We've had a request from her roommate's family. We have to ask. Her new roomie isn't sleeping well. Apparently your mother wanders and pulls at her oxygen tube and just generally doesn't settle down at night."

"Mom had to live through two ornery room-mates so let her new roomie live through Mom's shenanigan's, for gosh sakes." I hear how sharp my voice sounds but I do nothing to modulate it. "If Mom can look out her window even once more before she dies and see a familiar landscape then that's what I want her to be able to do. She loves her view and she'd lose it across the hall."

"We don't want to move her either. I just had to check. Don't worry, we're not going to move her."

"Thank you. If it's only for a second that she knows where she is. Thank you."

Herb and I come up on a Sunday. My brother and his wife have been to see our mother and they report that she is much as we find her, euphoric, confused, but generally not in pain. We get her into her wheel chair and the nurse attaches her portable oxygen tank to the back of the chair. I put a light robe over my mother's knees and we push her to the elevator. It is a beautiful early fall day and we will take her outside. "For a change of scene," I say to the nurse. Maybe it will be. Maybe Mom will respond to the fresh air and late blooming flowers.

I push her chair down the long paved slope of the front walk. We cross the driveway and walk along the path (paved with macadam so the wheelchairs and the walkers can proceed without trouble). We stop at a bench beside the rose garden and Herb and I sit close to my mother's chair. She does not have her hearing aids in. Something about getting them adjusted.

"Isn't this beautiful, Mom? Look at all the dahlias."

They are as tall as a ten-year-old child and their blooms are three and four inches across. Somebody here knows their stuff in the garden.

"Pretty," she says. "Big."

I smile at her but she is looking off over the hills in the distance.

"I'm very hungry. I don't think I've had anything to eat for a long time."

"It was lunch time when Herb and I came. Did you have lunch?"

She looks confused and a little angry.

"I don't know. I'm very hungry."

Herb goes back into the building and returns in a few minutes with a packet of peanut butter-and-cheese crackers, a can of Coke and a cup.

"How does this look, Mom?" he says, opening the crackers for her, holding one up for her to examine.

"Good," she says and takes the cracker from him, holds it up to her mouth, her hand shaking and crumbs falling over the front of her dress. She takes a bite, chews and swallows, smiles and says, "I was really hungry."

Her hands lie limp in her lap, the rest of the cracker falls from her grasp onto the ground beside her. I pull the zip top off the Coke and pour some into the paper cup.

"Some Coke, Mom? Crackers are dry all by themselves."

She leans forward to accept the rim of the cup with her dry lips, swallows once and says, "No more. I've over-eaten two times and it makes me feel sick. No more."

She is panting now, even with the oxygen.

"Let's go look at the flowers," I say, standing behind her chair. "We don't have to talk."

As we pass each rose bush, some in full bloom and some past prime, I lean to hold the stem of each to show her the heads of the flowers. She is silent and I'm not sure she's with us here in the garden.

Suddenly, she sits up straight, motions me to stop and says, "That's a tea rose. I know that, it's a tea rose." And it is.

There are no more phone calls to my mother. She doesn't hear the bell and the last time I called and the nurse gave her the phone she said, "I can't do this. Who is this?"

"Shirley," I said. "Your daughter."

"I can't think what you look like," she said.

"Well, I can think what you look like," I said. "You're a good looking old lady and you can think of me the same way."

She laughed and then was silent, breathing hard, gasping. Now I call the nurse's station to ask how she is and to say, "Give her a kiss for me." They always say they will and because I've seen how much they care for her, I know they will. The reports are more and more guarded. "She had a restless night but she's quiet now." "She had some soup this noon and some apple juice an hour or so ago." If Judy's on duty I get the real scoop. Judy loves my mother and she's having a hard time losing her. "Shirley, she won't stay in bed and she won't keep the oxygen on. Pulls it out of her nose. We're keeping her here at the station to keep an eye on her. She likes the bustle and seeing all the people. I think she hates to be left alone down there in her room."

The next Sunday Herb and I see the changes in her. She speaks less often and with less energy. Her words are sometimes slurred and the euphoria has gone. She's more focused and less content. She's busy dying.

CENTRAL PARK ZOO

Polar Bear

burlesque foot suctioned to the glass
he pushes off
swims on his back
clown paws resting on his chest
his fur suit
gaudy, white satin, beaded with silver strings of bubbles
sleek against his body
he slows to a float
black rubber nose straight up in the air
his white suit billows
blossoms
too big for him
made of stuff too fragile for a bear to wear
he looks ridiculous
we laugh out loud
calling him Polar Pagliacci
he grins his ursine grin to the sky above his pseudo glacier
a bear is swimming here, he says
if you thought it was a clown
it is because I chose to have you think so
come after dark to see the true bear
if you dare

82nd STREET OFF LEX IN JUNE

heat shimmered Serengeti sidewalk
dreadlocked lion glowers in the shade
tawny eyes sliding under heavy brows
flowered girls
and men with music on their shoulders
pass through his gaze
yellow taxis crawl by
honking and snarling
in the traffic river

he sees gazelles
giraffe and eland
hears the screech of carrion birds
and bides his time

ENCOUNTER IN FEBRUARY OUTSIDE THE CHURCH

Karen of the sorrows
you sit on the raw curb
arms around slender knees
cardboard coffee cup in one still hand
I slip futile coins into your cup
your young eyes smile
you rise and ask if I have been to mass
I say
how are you
are you alone
where is your family
you tell me of the shelter where you sleep
you touch my arm
and tell me to keep warm
I walk away
we call little words to one another
    across the growing space between
take care
stay warm

CITY FIX

we come in from the 'burbs
for our city fix
errands to be run
appointments to be kept
energy to be tapped
paintings and people to be seen
bus fumes and excitement to be inhaled
we come to test the connection
to our life support system

WATER STONE

Noguchi—1986

this black as basalt monk
squats on a bed of gravel
wearing a fluidsilver cloak
    closefitted as the night
silent, he asks me to see Alpha and Omega
Yin and Yang
the dark/light molecular dance
    of this ambivalent universe
in the stone of his waterbathed form

and, sometimes, I do

THE SLOTS

A Story

At eight that morning a big blue Cadillac with Helen Grady at the wheel stopped at the curb in front of the split ranch Louise and her late husband Edward had lived in for the forty years of their marriage. Edward's sudden death nearly a year before had left Louise more stunned than grieving. In life her husband had exuded the perfect confidence of a man whose ability to impose his will on others was all but uncontested. That gift had made him a solid middle level insurance salesman and it had assured Louise a life free of decision making. She had been content to follow where her pink cheeked, balding, dandy of a husband led. His sudden absence left her moving through her days in the pattern set by four decades of marriage, the object missing but the habits firmly in place. She continued to get up at seven, prepare a modest breakfast (one egg now instead of three), dust and vacuum the downstairs on Monday, the upstairs on Tuesday. On Wednesday she washed the few clothes and linens two people (now one person) soiled in one week and on Thursday she ironed those same clothes, no longer including Edward's shirts, his boxers and his pyjamas. On Friday Louise did the odds and ends of housekeeping, polishing the never tarnished silver, cleaning out the always neat refrigerator, sorting through the tidy closets, making order out of order. Saturday morning she accompanied her next door neighbor to the local Stop and Shop for the few necessities of her spare life. This pattern was for Louise, purpose. It served to get her up and dressed and left her ready for sleep by eleven in the evening. Some days she took a short nap after lunch. The nagging ache in her left hip and the shortness of breath she felt at the top of the stairs rode below her level of awareness most of the time and surfaced only in moments of fatigue or at the point of relaxation into sleep. She had said nothing to Edward about either thing nor had she mentioned them to Dr. Connor at her annual exam. Joints ached and breath grew short. That was life.

Now, as she stepped out onto the small porch, she turned to check the lock on the front door, turned back and walked toward the car. She saw that Jane Gurney and Isabel Freund were seated in the back seat. They had left the front passenger's side for her. She appreciated the nicety being extended to the new girl. The invitation had been to come with them to the casino today and if she had a good time they would be happy to have her join them in their twice monthly outings.

"Give it a shot, honey. You really need to get out," Isabel had said when she called to invite her. "Don't worry, we don't bet the rent money. We just have fun. A *lot* of fun."

She thought of the three women as acquaintances. They were people she saw at the super market or walking their dogs past her house. She and Edward had no real friends. He had said they were enough for each other without spending time and money sucking up to the neighbors. She had taken his word for it. Early in their marriage he had said the same about having children. The world was a tough place. He didn't make enough money. She'd be worn to a frazzle raising kids. Didn't she get tired just keeping the house and looking after him? She had taken his word for that, too.

She had been surprised and unsettled at Isabel's suggestion that she join them the following week for what she had called 'a present we all give ourselves a couple a' times a month'. The careful perimeter of her widowhood had been breached by someone who obviously thought she could function in the larger world. She had said she would think about it and had been amazed to find herself agreeing to go when Isabel declared she wasn't about to take *no*.

The ride took slightly more than an hour. Helen had a lead foot on the gas Edward had said the one time they rode with her to a Lion's picnic. Maybe so, but she drove confidently, with none of the speeding up, sudden slowing down, lane switches and foul language Louise was used to with her husband. Now the talk among the three friends was of poker machines, progressive betting, betting the limit and playing credit rather than coins for a faster game. Their words floated in the air around her. She couldn't pin them down long enough to decode them. 'Speaking in tongues,' she'd thought and kept silent, looking out the window at the clusters of houses, the gas stations and churches in the small towns they passed through, focusing on familiar objects.

Three weeks ago she had been taking a nap on the couch in the den with the TV turned low. She kept it on all day now that she was alone. Noise for company in the otherwise silent house. A loud voice exhorting her to "Take a chance! Be a winner!" had jarred her from the tag end of a dream. She had squinted at the image on the TV.

'I know that building. That's the casino Edward took me to the month before he died. What a place.'

The memory of the exotic, noisy space filled with machines and people disturbed her now as it had on that day. Edward had given her three rolls of quarters, ten dollars each, and told her to find a machine and have a good time. He would be at a black jack table and would come for her in a couple of hours. She was not to worry, he'd find her.

"Have fun," he'd said as he turned away.

It had been a command. She had watched Edward walk away and stood in the middle of the aisle between two banks of slot machines with more money in her hands to spend on utter foolishness than she had ever had in her life. Abandoned and weighted with the responsibility to enjoy herself, she had been confounded by the slot machine itself, had lost every quarter and been shamed by her ineptitude.

Sitting on the edge of the sofa, alone in her own home, she felt her cheeks flush at the image of the casino in full color on her television set, the sound of the voices urging her to take a chance, have some fun.

"Everybody wants me to have fun. It's a mystery to me how that's fun."

Now, in Helen's car, she wished she had brought her black leather purse. She needed to feel something solid and known. But Isabel had told her she would loan her a waist pack, that they all used them. She had dropped it off the day before, telling Louise, "Keeps your money close and your hands free. You'll get the hang of it. If you get to be a regular with us you can get one for yourself."

Louise had spent an anxious ten minutes that morning transferring her folded bills, a lipstick, a comb, a handkerchief, and her senior citizen identity card, from her purse to the navy blue canvas pouch of the waist pack. She had blushed as she fastened the grosgrain ribbon belt around her middle, over the waist band of her skirt and under her sweater. There was something about the intimate feel of the thing. She would have to see how the other women wore theirs. Over their blouses, under them, tight or slack. The subtle unspoken rules of dress and behavior distressed Louise in their complexity and this new wrinkle, this waist pack, was close to being too much of a challenge.

'I said I'd go and go I will,' she thought. "There's no one to tell me no. And no one to tell me if I look a fool in this thing, either," she said aloud, blousing her pale blue sweater to camouflage the lump the waist pack made.

She took a last look at herself in the full length mirror on the back of Edward's closet door and was satisfied she had done the best she could. The blue sweater complimented her eyes and her good gray skirt looked right with her white hair. Her low heeled black pumps were comfortable and neat. She *went together,* her mother's standard for the well dressed woman and the total catachism of style the quiet, careful woman had imparted to her daughter.

She walked down the carpeted stairs, holding on to the polished oak bannister. Her bifocals were treacherous on stairs. In the small front hall she put on her navy car coat.

'Oh, oh, almost forgot my key. Forget my head, sometimes.'

She opened the drawer of the half moon table that stood against the stair wall and took out a single brass key. Edward's heavy key chain with the enameled Lion's emblem and the six keys on its large ring was the only other object in the drawer. She knew his house key and the car key but what the other four opened she didn't know and didn't care. His key ring could stay where it was, but seeing it had brought Edward to mind in a way she had been avoiding. What would he think of her intention to squander three hundred dollars? It hadn't been *his* idea, after all. Edward hadn't been mean with money but he did write all the checks. Her name was not on the checking account. "Gotta keep a tight hold on those purse strings." She had been on an allowance all their married life. Not a generous amount but enough to keep the house running and her wardrobe in decent shape. At the time of their marriage he had opened a savings account for her into which he deposited one hundred dollars each quarter. Her butter and egg money, he called it. The amount had not changed over the years of their marriage so that what had been seen by her as a generous and loving gift to a new bride became something less than that over time. She had never asked for more but had begun to put away a dollar here and five dollars there as she could wriggle it out of the household money. Clipping coupons, serving stew instead of chops now and then. Edward liked her stew. He never questioned her handling of the household money. In this way she was able to keep what she thought of as a repectable amount in her account.

When he died she found he had left her enough money to see her through twenty years or more of moderate living.

"There's enough for you to live comfortably, Louise. Not high on the hog but if you're careful you'll be fine," Ted Fielding, their lawyer, had said.

Not high on the hog. Not putting three hundred dollars into a machine that would give her nothing back.

She shook her head, slid the house key into the side pocket of her coat and glanced into the bull's eye mirror on the wall beside the front door to check her hair and lipstick.

"Once. I'll do it just this once."

She opened her coat, put her right hand over the bulge at her waist and petted it twice, as she would have stroked a cat.

That morning she had gone to the bank, stood before the ATM machine and realized she had no idea how to proceed. To have gone into the bank as usual and put her withdrawal slip on the counter in front of any of the tellers, people who knew her, was not something she could do for this particular transaction. She used this account for extra expenses, a special gift to the church of fifty dollars at Christmas, her birthday and Christmas gifts to Edward. A few small withdrawals each year. The amount she intended to take out on this day, three hundred dollars, might cause the teller to question her.

"Are you sure, Mrs. Waring? You didn't mean to write *thirty* dollars, did you?"

She had heard of older women being duped into cashing large amounts of money by scam artists. Tellers would be alert to this possibility. She would brave the ATM rather than have a confrontation of the kind she imagined. She inserted her bank card, read the message on the monitor and followed the directions slowly and meticulously to the obvious annoyance of the tall, impatient young man waiting behind her.

She stood with her back firmly to the young man whose exhaled sighs barely registered in her consciousness and took hold of the thick sheaf of twenties that were fed from the machine. She counted them out, slowly, carefully, onto the small shelf below the machine, then folded them and placed them in the zippered pocket of her purse. She became aware of the question the monitor was asking, had been asking since it growled out her money. "Do you want another transaction?" She pressed *no*. "Do you want a written receipt?" She pressed *yes* and waited for the printed record to emerge from the slot, took it without registering the blue ink record of her folly, put it in her purse and snapped the clasp closed. She hurried out of the bank, across the street and down the block to the bus stop and was home again in fifteen minutes.

She put her purse in the top drawer of her bureau and went down to the kitchen to brew a pot of tea. From the moment she had decided to withdraw the money and go to the casino her heart had been pounding in her throat. The decision had kept her from sleeping and she was a sound sleeper. It had quelled her always moderate appetite. Now she would sit quietly for half an hour, sip her tea, and allow this thing that she had done to become ordinary, something she could expect from herself in her widowed circumstance. A half hour later she began to breath more evenly. Her heart took up its usual rhythm. She did not sleep well that night but she put her insomnia down to excitement over the adventure of the coming day.

Helen Grady had offered to pick her up for the ride to the casino. Louise did not have a driver's license. Edward's car (she had never thought of it as *their* car) stood in the garage waiting for her to make up her mind to sell it. To have put an ad in the local paper or indeed to have asked Edward's friend Howard at the used car lot to sell it for her was too much like usurping her husband's place. The car could sit there forever as far she was concerned. She had never wanted to learn to drive and had been happy to have Edward chauffeur her.

"Leave the driving to me," he would say, laughing the short, sharp laugh that meant he was enjoying his own joke, his take on the Greyhound ad. Edward bragged about his sense of humor.

"You couldn't make a joke to save your life, could you, honey? Never mind, I need you to laugh at my jokes," he said. Often. She didn't always get the point of what he called his puns but she always laughed.

Since his death she hadn't laughed at anything and hadn't missed it.

At exactly nine fifteen Helen had parked, expertly and with a flourish of the steering wheel, in one of the casino parking lots a good five long blocks from the entrance to the building. She had said to Louise, "We go our separate ways inside. Everybody has their own way of doing this thing. We'll meet up for a bite at the Odds On Buffet about four thirty and then we can play for another hour or so. I'll get us home early enough. That suit you okay?"

"Fine," Louise said, thinking, 'What on God's green earth am I going to do for all those hours? I should've asked how long they stayed. Well, I've done it now.'

"Have fun," Edward had said but that was when he was in charge, when he had given her the thirty dollars. She felt hot tears and closed her eyes against them. Not tears for Edward but in the certain knowledge that she was out of her depth.

Louise stood beside the car waiting for the others to indicate their pleasure. She was over dressed. All three women were in slacks or jeans and sneakers, their waist packs worn over their sweaters or shirts, hanging low in front over their stomachs. None of the women wore coats. She had asked if Helen would be warm enough in her thin argyle sweater worn over a man tailored shirt.

"You don't want the hassle of keeping track of a coat. The air conditioning keeps the place comfortable."

"Air conditioning?" Louise asked.

"Conditioned air, really. One temperature all the time. Keeps you at the machines longer if you're comfortable. They filter the air, too, so the smoking doesn't bother you. Seems like everybody smokes. Here, I'll unlock the trunk so you can leave your coat if you want."

Helen reached into the trunk, picked up a beach towel from a heap of bathing suits and towels obviously left there from last summer and laid it across the tool chest and the spare tire.

"That should do it, Lou."

Louise shrugged off her coat, folded it lining side out and placed it on the towel. She stepped back as Helen closed the trunk and took the moment to look up at the huge sandstone building at the top of the crest. The tall old growth trees that were shown in all the ads were there but they were hundreds of yards from the green expanse of lawn manicured to wedding cake perfection on which the casino sat. Great panes of aquamarine glass set in walls across the twenty story facade reflected the sky and tinted the few fair weather clouds the green of an alien atmosphere.

'I like things their natural color,' Louise thought. 'Looks like the Emerald City, for heaven's sake. I don't remember noticing that when Edward and I were here.'

"No sense having to tip for valet parking," Helen said. "We always walk up to the main entrance." She paused and added, "Or we can wait for the jitney if it's too far for you."

"No, no, I'm happy to walk."

She took a couple of steps and found she could walk without favoring her left hip, stiffened from the hour in the car. She took a deep breath and walked off after the other three women. They went quickly, single file, up the long drive to the porticoed entrance, Isabel, her shoulder length faded red hair streaming behind her, in the lead.

"She has to get a spot at *her* Black Jack table," Helen turned back to Louise to say. "She swears she's going to win enough for a new refrigerator."

"She told me this was just for fun. That you don't bet the rent money," Louise said, catching her breath to keep up with Helen.

"Oh, it is. It is. For fun. We always hope we'll hit a big payoff, though. You know how it is."

Jane and Isabel had gone into the lobby by the time Helen and Louise reached the row of heavy glass doors at the entrance to the building. Helen stepped up to the center door, grasped the huge brass handle and held the door open for Louise.

"You okay on your own now? Want me to stay with you for a while till you're acclimated?" Helen asked as she followed Louise into the lobby.

"No thanks, Helen. Edward and I were here last year. I'll find my way all right. You go on ahead and I'll see you all at the restaurant later."

Louise stood just inside the entrance to the two story marble lobby watching Helen stride off across the highly polished floor to catch up with Jane and Isabel. She watched them disappear into the arched entrance of the casino nearly three long blocks from where she stood. She studied the marble pillars, the overstuffed chairs placed in groups of three and four, the tall lamps of forged metal with blown glass shades that sent the light searching into the dark upper reaches, and the discrete marble desks marked REGISTRATION, CHECK OUT, and GUEST SERVICES placed at the far edges of the lobby so as not to introduce business directly into the walk from entrance to casino. She had thought simply that the place was over done when she was here the first time. Over done, over dressed. Now she thought that perhaps the lushness, the size, the high polish, the richness of fabric and marble was not unlike Christmas decorations in department store windows. She wouldn't want the tinsel and glitter around all year. It was cloying. But the fake fir trees, the figures of angels and reindeer, the mulicolored lights, did add something to the anticipation even she felt, childless and without much to look forward to beyond a midnight visit to church on Christmas Eve and a roast chicken dinner with Edward on Christmas Day. Here in this place she felt that same heightened anticipation. Everything larger than life. No one in the real world had chairs that size, lamps that tall, pillars in their living rooms.

"It's exciting," she thought.

The insistent whirring note coming from somewhere above and permeating the air around her she had remembered as annoying. Edward had said that it was the sound of slot machines piped into the lobby from the the casino itself in order to 'get your juices flowing the minute you put foot in the place. Suckers game.' But today it seemed ethereal, a sound she might have expected to hear in a cathedral.

Louise took a breath and walked across the lobby in the direction of the arch through which Helen and the other two women had disappeared. She walked carefully, conscious of the clicking of the metal taps on the heels of her black pumps against the marble floor. Edward had insisted she have taps put on the heels of all her shoes. "Adds years. Money out the window to wear your heels down."

The laughter of two women sitting opposite one another in a pair of the oversized chairs caught her attention. The women, one bright with jewelry and impossibly golden hair, the other round and lavender gray, were gesturing, interrupting one another, laughing, comfortable together and in their surroundings. Louise walked slower, looked hard at the women who were too engrossed in one another to notice her stare. There were two large cardboard cups on the low table between the women.

'Coffee,' Louise thought, wishing she had a small cup of her own. Breakfast seemed a long time ago.

'Not coffee. Quarters.'

She remembered now that on a shelf beside each slot machine was a pile of cardboard cups for the taking. They were to hold one's winnings or the quarters one was using to feed the machines. On her previous visit she had not won nor spent enough to bother with a cup but she had seen how they were used. Each of the cups on the coffee table was filled to the brim with quarters. Louise had no idea what that might be in dollars but she was sure it was enough to account for the note of celebration she heard in the women's laughter.

She walked on, swinging her arms now, less cautious. The clicking of her heels was, she realized, lost to all ears but her own in the noise of the slot machines, the humming note that grew louder as she approached the casino. The opening through which she passed had been daunting when she was here with Edward. The pedestal sign reading "No Person Under the Age of Twenty One Years May Enter the Casino Under Penalty of the Law" and placed where it could not be missed, the uniformed guard standing at ease to one side of the entrance, had been threatening. Today she was curious and excited. She glanced at the sign and at the guard, a man whom she took to be about her own age, who smiled and said, "Good luck, maam." She thanked him and walked in to the brightly lit, noisy space. The banks of machines each with its own graphics, its own icons, each with its own sound of metal drums revolving, of electronic voices calling out "You're a winner" or "Try again", each with its own player seated on a stool in front of it feeding it coins one after the other, were as she remembered. The memory itself, this feeling of familiarity, encouraged her to begin looking for a vacant stool in front of a slot machine. Any machine, she thought at first. Then she began to study the names that appeared in bright graphics above each chrome and glass front: "Roaring Twenties" with a picture of Betty Boop, "Lucky Seven", "Triple Twist", "Bingo Blaster". Some showed three lines of icons when the reels were spun and had three black lines across the face of the glass display. Some had five black lines, three horizontal and two diagonal. Some appeared to be poker hands with cards appearing and disappearing as the player touched any of a row of buttons mounted below the glass face. What on earth? When she was here before she simply sat on a stool and fed quarters into the slot. Now she wanted to understand what she was choosing when she finally made the decision to sit. She wanted to understand how the machine worked, what it wanted of her and what her chances might be of getting something back, of not throwing her entire three hundred dollars away. Her intense focus on the possibilities of each of the shiny, whirring machines tightened the muscles of her back and neck. A headache began behind her eyes. Nothing came clear beyond the obvious. She would find a vacant seat and would begin to feed her money into whatever machine chance placed before her, just as she had done before.

She walked down the wide center aisle looking first left and then right at the banks of machines arrayed in rows on either side. All were in use by white haired men and women, balding men, women who had settled on blonde bee hive hair dos forty years before and had found no reason to change in the intervening decades, younger men in jeans whose tee shirts advertised beer or proclaimed that the wearer was of Italian or Irish ancestry and should be kissed, middle aged Asian women, tidy in their black jackets and slacks or smart sweat suits, their demeanor business like and serious except for the occasional burst of behind the hand laughter when the machine they were playing paid off in a loud cascade of coins. Here and there a stool had been removed by one of the many uniformed attendants in order to accomodate a customer using one of the motorized wheel chairs made available by the casino. Louise would take the first empty seat that presented itself.

She had walked a third of the way across the casino when she spotted an idle machine second in on the row to her right. She walked over and sat down, her eyes lowered, her gaze avoiding the person on her left and the person on her right. After a long moment she raised her eyes and began to study the instructions on her machine.

"25 Cents"

"Play Three Coins"

Did she have to play three quarters each time? If so her money would go very quickly.

"Machine Error Nullifies all Play and Payoff"

"Credit/Pay"

She remembered that one. If you had a winner you pushed that button to release your payoff quarters into the tray below. The credit part she did not understand.

"Machine Accepts $10, $20, $50, $100"

Accepts money? For what? When she had been here before Edward had provided her with quarters. This time she had not thought beyond getting her money from the bank. Had not thought to change the bills to quarters. This sign had to mean that the machine would change her twenties. She slid the zipper open on her waist pack, felt the wad of money, separated one twenty from the rest without looking down and zipped the pack closed. If she didn't call attention to her three hundred dollars no one would be tempted to relieve her of it.

She studied the space below the dollar amounts and found a horizontal slit. She placed one narrow end of the crisp bill into the slit, face up as the diagram above the slit requested, and felt the machine tug it from her grasp. Her twenty disappeared and nothing happened. She sat looking at the face of the machine, embarassed. What should she do? Had she misunderstood? Maybe the machine just kept her money if she were foolish enough to feed it. Her right hand moved up to the face of the machine, her fingers looking for the answer. Her index finger pressed "Credit/Pay" and a torrent of quarters clanked into the tray before her. A small window marked "PAID" lit up and the number 80 appeared. Of course. "Pay" 80 quarters for twenty dollars. She reached for a cardboard cup from the supply on the shelf beside the machine and began scooping up her coins and placing them in the cup. She held the cup against her chest and the weight of it was warm and reassuring.

Louise reached in and took out a quarter. She slipped it into the coin slot and pressed the button that said SPIN REELS. The machine whirred into life. The pictures on the three reels behind the glass face of the machine moved down and around and were replaced by other images. A red seven, a pot of gold, a heart became three palm trees. A thin black horizontal line ran across the window bisecting each tree. The PAY button lit up. Louise sat back on the stool and studied the three palm trees. She had won. Something. Some amount of quarters. On her first try. The window that had told her she had 80 quarters for her twenty dollar bill now said 15. She pushed the PAY button and coins clattered into the tray.

"Fifteen quarters," she said aloud as she counted them into her cup. "How much is that in money?"

Three dollars and seventy five cents for a quarter.

From her right she heard a man's voice, low and deep. Self-mocking.

"My last dime. Make that my last quarter. Well, here goes nothin'."

Without turning to look at the speaker Louise heard the machine next to hers accept a coin, heard the reels spin, heard the repeated upward whoop of a machine about to pay off, heard her neighbor say, "Hit it, by God. Four hundred dollars. Holy shit, about time."

Louise swung her stool to the right and was surprised to see that the young man, the big winner, was looking directly at her, including her in his good fortune.

"Have to wait for one of the guys to pay off," he said shrugging at the machine.

The frosted glass cylinder light perched on top of the machine was lit and blinking. The whooping sound continued, loud and impersonal as a car alarm.

"A thousand quarters or more they have to come pay you. The machines aren't set up for that big a hit," he said, explaining, teaching.

"Congratulations," Louise said and turned back to her own machine.

She had taken in the young man's thin, sharp face, his water-blue eyes, his hair, a color her mother had called dirty blond, and the pale stubble on his chin and cheeks. Now she saw from the corner of her eye his denim clad leg stretched out nearly into her space, his surprisingly small foot in its clean white athletic sneaker toe-tapping against the base of his machine, and his left hand resting on his leg, long yellowed fingers holding the stub of a cigarette, smoke rising and then disappearing into the cool air, sucked away by whatever system kept the huge space comfortable. She felt the presence of someone standing behind her. The young man stood and began talking to the new arrival, an attendant in a maroon jacket.

A moment later the young man leaned over her shoulder and said, "You'd get more pay offs if you played all three lines. Three quarters each time. Play the limit. Mind watching my machine for me while I cash out?"

"What do I say if someone wants to sit there?"

"I'll leave my jacket on the seat. Just say your husband will be back in a minute."

An hour had passed and forty minutes of a second hour since she had said "You're welcome" to the young man when he had thanked her for minding his machine, picked up his jacket and walked away down the center aisle of the casino, his hips swaying to the winner's inner rhythm and she had begun playing three quarters at a time.

'At this rate I'll be out of money before I meet the girls for supper.'

She had laid her hand over her waist pack and thought, 'In for a penny.'

Now she sat back on her stool, her back and legs tight with fatigue and with the tension of leaning forward into the work of feeding coins into the slot. Two cups filled with quarters sat tucked into the niche to the right of her machine. She had lost track of her total winnings but she knew she now had more money than she had brought with her. Maybe as much as fifty dollars more. She felt a trancelike comfort at the thought. Soothed by the sight and the feel of the coins.

What now disturbed her peace was a sudden urge to get to a bathroom. Where were the rest rooms? Silly not to have asked when she came in. She always located a ladies room when she was in new surroundings. What would she do with the two heavy cups? Must she give up her machine? The woman in the turqouise pant suit sitting to her right at what Louise thought of as Denim Jacket's machine was playing credits as fast as she could push the button. She had not looked away from her work since she sat down. Louise felt she would not take kindly to a request to save her place. Would another machine be as lucky? Pay off as handsomely and as dependably as this one was doing? She realized she would have to take the chance. As she stood, awkwardly, grasping the top of the machine to steady herself, her hip threatened not to hold her weight.

'Too long in one position,' she thought. 'What on earth was I thinking?'

Louise spotted the REST ROOMS sign, far down the right hand side of the huge room past the cashiers' cages. She hugged the two heavy cups of coins to her waist with both hands and started off.

On impulse she stopped in front of the first cashier, a tanned-to-leather young woman with laquered blond hair and a friendly smile, and asked, "Is this where I . . . ?"

"Yes. maam, right here. Just put your cups right up here."

Louise hefted her winnings onto the counter and watched as the cashier dumped them into a coin counting machine mounted beside her. The machine clanked and whirred. The total appeared in a small framed window on the edge of the coin counter. The cashier's short, scarlet nails clicked against the marble of the counter as she flicked six crisp twenty dollar bills into a pile in front of Louise.

"One hundred twenty dollars and fifty cents," she said, sliding two quarters across the counter. "Thank you, maam. Have a lucky day."

"I am having a very lucky day, thank you very much," Louise said, picking up the quarters first and then the pile of bills.

She took two steps away from the counter, turned toward the tan marble wall away from the eyes of the people passing and slid open the zipper on her waist pack. She took one twenty dollar bill and folded it and placed it beside her original packet of twenties.

'Just exactly what I started with,' she thought. 'And a hundred more. I can't believe it.'

She folded the five twenties and slipped them into the narrow on seam pocket on the left side of her skirt.

'I can play for days on that hundred at the rate I'm going.'

As she entered an empty stall in the rest room she caught sight of her right hand.

"My gosh, I'm filthy," she said aloud.

Her fingers were stained a dark grey, greasy to the feel and as repulsive as blood to Louise. She ignored the intense need to urinate and backed out of the stall, walked over to a sink and wet her hands under the automatic-on faucet.

"You gotta use that soap there," the woman at the next sink offered, indicating the chrome pump set into the marble counter beside the faucet. "That stuff is the devil to get off. From the money. Filthy lucre. Lots of 'em play credits just so they don't get their hands dirty but I like the feel of the quarters, don't you? Makes it real. Come often?"

"No, it's my first time," Louise said, pumping liquid soap into her left palm, rubbing her hands together to make a lather, looking into the mirror, first at herself and then at the woman who had spoken. She saw a large gray haired woman in a paisley dress, tight across the bust and under the arms, smiling at her, yellowed dentures revealed both top and bottom like a dental mold or a skull.

"Any luck? Beginners luck, I'll bet. Am I right?"

Louise rinsed the soap from her hands and reached for one of the folded paper towels from the stack on the counter. She began to dry her hands as she turned from the sink to face the woman.

"I have had some luck as it happens."

"I knew it. It never fails. But you can only be a beginner once, right?"

The woman made the sound of a laugh but Louise heard no humor in it. One of those laughs people use to punctuate small talk.

"Excuse me," Louise said and walked back into the stall she had vacated moments before.

She pulled a paper toilet seat cover from the dispenser on the wall above the toilet and covered the seat carefully. She let herself down slowly, holding on to the chrome bar provided above the toilet tissue holder.

'Nice,' she thought.

The relief of urinating relaxed her, made her sleepy. She realized she had missed her nap. And lunch. She was startled to hear the woman's voice through the stall door, loud enough to sound hollow in the marble rest room.

"You here alone? You want company?"

"I came with some lady friends," Louise said in a modulated voice, embarrassed at speaking from her place on the toilet. "We're going to meet up at the Buffet later." Regretting her mention of the Buffet. Maybe this woman would take it as an invitation to join them.

"Oh, good. I thought you might be alone. I'm on my way, then. Nice talkin' to ya'. Good luck."

Louise sat on in the privacy of the stall, listening to the woman's retreating footsteps. The realization that this woman thought Louise might have made the decision to spend the day at the casino and come here alone, without a husband, needed thinking about. She stood and spent another minute arranging her skirt, adjusting her waist pack. She looked at her watch and realized she had more than an hour before she had to find the Odds On Buffet. Her heart gave a series of quick beats. Time enough to find another machine and see what might happen. She walked from the stall, went to the sink and washed her hands again. She looked into the huge mirror that gave back her trim, gray haired, blue eyed self, ran her fingers through her hair, touched the pocket of her skirt with the tips of the fingers of her left hand, and smiled.

'I can take lessons. I can learn to drive the car,' she thought.

She took the polished brass handle of the heavy rest room door in her right hand, pulled the door open and walked out into the casino

PARROT

the parrot's ballbearing eye
stares me down
unblinking steel

emerald and ruby feathers
jeweled disguise
for the coldest heart in the tropics

HOCUS POCUS

the cat has a cut over her eye
it's new and it's deep
she never leaves the house
we did not throw her against the radiator
no one came into the house and bit her
the house is not, so far as we know, haunted
she licks her yellow paw and rubs it over the cut
again and again and again
in two days the cut has disappeared
the cat is not surprised
neither is she grateful for this healing
she yearns at the window
the birds at the feeder are safe in their feathers
from her needle claws
until she learns the paw-through-the-glass trick

FOR GRACE AT HER EASEL

from two dimensions
three
and more

you show me what you see
and more
you show me who you are

MEMOIR OF A RELUCTANT PSYCHIC

When I was a child and under the tutelage of my mother's mother I was what she called 'sensitive' to people. Not all the time but often enough for her to think I had *the gift*. Then and now I misjudge and devalue and overvalue people all the time, but when the focus kicks in, I'm pretty good. Most of the time it's a matter of will. I decide when I will read palms or hold a séance. Often I do it just because I'm asked, but if the focus isn't there, if the doubts are stronger than the impulse, the answer will be *no*. I'm now in my seventies and until recently the answer has been *no* for long years, for reasons which will become clear.

For my grandmother it was easy. Or I thought so. It seemed so. She would brew a pot of loose-leaf tea, fill my cup one third with the steaming liquid, take the top off the pot and spoon some of the soggy leaves into my cup.

"Sip it slowly. Think about what you want to know as you sip. When the tea is gone, turn the cup upside down on your saucer, the handle toward you. Turn the cup three times around and lift it up. Don't you look at it. Hand it to me."

I would do exactly as she said, the china cup rasping against the saucer. I could never drink all of the tea, never get the cup really drained before upending it. The final drops always ran down inside the curve, puddling in the saucer.

She would take the cup from me, her hands white as old linen, blue veined and fragile. She would stare into the cup for long seconds and then smile.

"This is a good one, honey. See that bouquet of flowers in the bottom?" holding the cup tilted toward me and pointing with her pinkie at the wet tea leaves clustered at the bottom. I nodded 'yes' and she went on.

"Happy times are coming for you. Maybe not next week but soon. Really happy times."

That much was wish as much as prophecy, for all of us, I know now. But her next words came from her gift.

"And a party. I see a party for someone whose name begins with B. Is that right? Betty? Barbara?"

Planned children's parties weren't all that common in those days. The Depression was deep and wide and we made our fun from the simple, spontaneous things we found around us. The week after my grandmother's reading I was invited to a birthday party for Betty, a classmate. Betty's party, planned on purpose and including me, was important enough to have shown up in my tea leaves.

My mother and my little brother showed little interest in my grandmother's readings. My girl cousins were as fascinated as I, but my brother ignored them. As an adult I would discover that he found her 'spiritualism' as he defined it, unholy, and therefore to be despised. Not our grandmother herself but her delving into what he perceived as witchcraft. But I understood that she knew things that others did not, that she believed what she knew, and that I, too, had feelings and thoughts that were at odds with my generally practical nature. I wanted to know all that she could teach me.

I wanted her to read my palm. Tea leaves were fun, but the real things were revealed in the palm, so she always said. She would finally agree to read my hand but always with a strong caveat.

"You're too young to have your fortune read. You haven't been alive long enough to take charge of your life. I can tell you what gifts you were born with but I can't tell you how you're going to use them. Reading family is tricky anyway. I know you too well."

"Please, Gram, please," I would beg, impatient to get on with it, whatever 'it' was. I was eight or ten or twelve and life was taking too long to get somewhere. She would take my left hand, cradle it, palm up in her own warm palm and study the all but invisible childhood lines.

"You're smart, Shirley. Really smart. And stubborn. My word, you are stubborn."

She knew these things about me without looking at my hand, but she was so intense when she spoke that what she said had another meaning. 'She's seeing into me. It's not just what she knows because she's my grandma.'

"You let the *stubborn* get in the way of the *smart* sometimes."

She would turn my hand to see along the outer edge.

"You will have children. I see one, no, two. One is not so clear but it's there. And one marriage. Good."

I have had one marriage. We have celebrated more than fifty years together. We have two children, an adopted daughter and a son.

I was not surprised that I had a 'knack' for palmistry and for what I came to think of as character reading. It seemed a natural outgrowth of the time I spent with Grandma Rough. I had not yet begun to question the apparent divergence from my usual logical thought.

I started reading palms in my early teens. At first it was a gimmick, a way to get attention. I liked being in the limelight and palm reading put me there. I would say all the obvious things. "You will meet a really nice boy at the next dance." The kids who went to the dances were all from the town school. The chances of there being a strange and wonderful new boy at any of them were all but nil, still the subject of my reading would tell her friends, "Shirley says I'll meet a new boy." The fact that this did not happen didn't dampen anybody's enthusiasm for my readings.

As time went on I began to grow into the feeling of holding someone's hand in mine, of letting my mind focus and of saying what came to my lips: "What is the problem with your father? Is he sick? Is he angry with you?"

To another: "You have a lot of talent in, I think it's art. Do you know that?"

And: "You're a very loving person, but you don't show it much. People can't guess what you're like, you have to let them see."

By the time I was in college I was getting the hang of it. I was beginning to forget about the 'heart line' and the 'life line'. I still told people about them because that's what they expected, but the real stuff was coming clear. Not that I had to do anything special, just focus on the person who placed his or her hand in mine. Some of the hands were hot and dry and stiff, not trusting, not believing. Some were moist and limp, fingers curled in like a wilting flower. Inert, impassive. Tell me what you will, they said. Some were strong, like a good handshake. Confident and healthy. I took my cues from what was presented, but it was always more than that. If the person would let me, I could cross the space between us to get inside, through the eyes, through the skin, through the blood. But, like hypnosis, if the person did not want to let me in I was stymied and I would say so.

"I can't do a good reading for you. It would be unfair to try."

Those people never pushed for more. They knew what I knew. No way in. Or out.

I had bad feelings at times. Forebodings of illness or death, serious trouble of some kind. I would back off from that, keep it to myself. Grandma did the same. "There's enough trouble in the world without having people worry about something I've said."

Occasionally someone would sense that I was fudging and would ask what was wrong.

"Nothing," I would say. "Just some things aren't quite clear to me."

So I couldn't tell the awful things. They would come clear when they actually happened. And I didn't take money for readings. There was not then and is not now any logical reason for my refusal of money. People offered to pay me when I was at college and could have used the extra dollar or two. Instead I washed and cut the other students' hair for twenty-five or thirty cents. Movie money.

I don't know why I looked for logical explanations for anything to do with the readings. Nothing about the *feelings* will yield to intellectual examination. I use the clues people send out in my presence, true. I use intuition, whatever that may be. Probably true. The word I choose to use is inference. I'm good at drawing inferences, true. But it's more than that. Greater than the sum of those parts. What happens in a really good reading is connection. I *am* the person I am reading.

The good readings pose problems. On the one hand I am in total control. I'm the boss, the guru, the crone. Great feeling. At the same time the intensity of the experience takes over and I become the messenger. That's what makes it a good reading. It is one reason I have stayed away from such things for so long. My brain resists the giving over of my rational self to whatever comes through me. The ambiguity is intensely uncomfortable.

Grandma Rough did séances, too. and I learned from her. She would draw the curtains or pull down the blinds, turn off the radio and the lights, and place one lighted candle in the center of the dining room or kitchen table. Whoever was in the house at the time—aunts, uncles, cousins, friends—would gather around the table in the semi dark.

"Look at the candle. Keep your eyes on it. Try not to blink," she would say in her séance voice, quiet, controlled, imperative. You really tried hard not to blink.

"Hold hands, please. Firm but not tight. Make your mind a blank."

There would be some shuffling of feet on the linoleum floor, some shifting in the wooden kitchen chairs and then silence. Silence was hard for my uncle. He would peer at us from under his lowered brow and try to make us laugh. But his mother, my grandmother, would wait him out and finally there would be silence, a long silence.

"Someone wants to tell us that everything is forgiven. Does that mean anything to anyone? All is forgiven."

A neighbor woman, old and rather cross most of the time, claimed the message.

"Yes, it's my father," she said in a small voice. "He died before we had a chance to make up the fight."

Often the message would be greeted by silence, would lie there in the shadows, unclaimed. But Grandma Rough was undaunted. She understood that some words might be too powerful, too personal, to be recognized in the company of others.

There was skepticism in my family about what my grandmother did. My mother had, through natural inclination and through the circumstances of her life, become a pragmatic adult, living in the moment and dealing with life as it happened. She appreciated the fantasy of children's minds, their stories and poems, and there were occasions when she would say "I have a feeling—". When she held her first grandchild, our infant daughter, in her arms she said, "She's an old soul. She knows more than we do." Still, the practical prevailed and she was skeptical of her mother's gift.

My father was an inventor and a pilot in the earliest days of flying. He dreamed large dreams but they were of gas engines and electric motors and airplanes built by his own hand. They did not include anything that could not be made to work in the concrete world.

My grandmother's real world included two failed marriages and four children. My mother was the second oldest after Kenneth, the first born and the farthest removed geographically. Third in line was Martha, sweet natured, mother of four herself, and dying for most of her adult life of multiple sclerosis. Rink, the youngest, had put out one of his eyes with a knife when he was four, trying to open a Christmas package. It was he who tried to make us laugh during séance and he who *would* make us laugh for all of his short life. There was never enough money, even for basics. That condition was not peculiar to my grandmother. It was the Great Depression and everyone scrambled to keep warm and to put food on the table. Grandma looked for beauty everywhere, in the dime store trinkets she could sometimes afford and in the pansies in her garden. And, I have no doubt, she found it in allowing herself to go wherever she was led in her readings. Freedom from worry, freedom to be her most private self. I was the only one who was willing and eager to follow her.

Yet I, too, am a pragmatist. I love the proving of a supposition by logic. Or the disproving. I love the building of a thing from idea to finished product whether I do it myself or enjoy someone else's efforts. A house, the Suez Canal, a fort of children's blocks, a space station or a birthday cake. Still I was fascinated by what my grandmother called 'the occult', the hidden revealed.

There was an incident when I was twelve that became the touchstone for me. I couldn't then nor can I now discount it nor explain it.

We had moved, my parents, my brother and I, to California for my father's health. He had severe asthma and at thirty-seven was desperate to find a place where he could breathe. We had lived in Burbank for six months when one sunny December day he stayed home from work, lay in bed in his oxygen tent, and, with my mother lying beside him and my brother and me in the living room with our Aunt Mildred and Uncle Charles, he died. We took the four day train trip home to Connecticut with my father's casket in the baggage car. On arrival we went immediately to live in the huge family home of my father's mother, Nana Williams. My father's sister and her husband and three daughters were living there but the estate was large enough to accommodate three more without dispossessing anyone. We settled in to our new surroundings on the third floor without comment or discussion. There was no money. My father's health had precluded life insurance and the end of the Depression found my mother without savings, so this place, the Farm as the family called it, would be home to my mother, my brother and me for the foreseeable future. My father was buried from the Farm two days after we moved in.

Grandma Rough lived in a small frame house in the same town. My unmarried uncle, fragile aunt, and two cousins lived with her in what can best be described as the near edge of poverty. I know now how strong a contrast existed between the homes and the lives of my two grandmothers, but at the time the only important thing was that they both loved me.

A week or so after the funeral, I had a weekend visit with my mother's family. I sat opposite Grandma Rough at her kitchen table over a cup of cocoa and a wedge of her walnut coffee cake.

"I have to tell you something, Shirley. I've been wanting to talk to you since your Daddy's funeral. I'm still trying to believe what happened."

I thought she was referring to my father's sudden death. They had not had a comfortable relationship. Polite but not warm. I hoped she was not going to tell me she was relieved that he was gone. At twelve such a thing seemed possible but I did not want to hear it.

Instead, she began telling me about the week leading up to my father's death. It had been a hard week for her. She had no money for coal and she feared that my aunt, frail as she was, would take cold or pneumonia in the frigid house. On the day my father died and with no knowledge that he was ill, she went down to the cellar to scrape up what loose pieces of coal, even coal dust, she might find to stoke the boiler. As she stood at the entrance to the coal bin she saw my father standing against the back wall, his head tipped to the side, a smile on his face. She saw his red hair, his mustache, his tweed jacket, as clear as day, even in the shadows of the coal bin.

"Looking jaunty as always," she said to me. "Not in the least sick or unhappy. His own self. 'Don't worry, Florence,' was what he said. Just that. 'Don't worry, Florence.' And I stopped worrying right then. The boiler cold and dead, Martha huddled under blankets on her bed, and I stopped worrying. In the next minute your father wasn't there. Not disappeared so much as . . . I don't know how to say it . . . faded into nothing."

"So I went upstairs and continued on right through the dining room and out the front door to the mail box. I'd checked for mail about an hour before and there hadn't been anything. But this time there was an envelope, a letter addressed to me in your father's handwriting. He never wrote to me. Never called me up. We weren't on the best of terms as I guess you know. I opened the envelope right there at the edge of the road, my fingers so cold I could hardly manage, and there it was."

What she pulled from the envelope was a sheet of lined paper folded over a check for twenty-five dollars. A week's pay for many in those days. An enormous gift. He had written a Christmas greeting on the sheet of paper. "A little early Christmas. Love from Bertie, Jim and the kids." Grandma said she went straight to the telephone, called the coal company and they were warm and cozy until well into the new year.

"When your mother called to tell us about your father dying I figured it out. The time difference, I mean. Your Dad was with me just minutes after he died."

I never talked about it with her again but I never forgot a word of it. Not logical, not concrete, not provable, but true and so much bigger than tea leaves or séances.

My family was tolerant of my interest in learning what Grandma had to teach. "Oh, those two," with a dismissive smile. The year after my grandmother died I met and married Herb. I found that there was another way of dealing with my interest in things occult, my husband's way. Herb had no frame of reference for such things and he didn't believe for a moment that I could 'see' things or that my 'feelings' were anything but a manifestation of attention to inference. But he appreciated the way people responded to my palm readings. It was an amusing parlor trick, one he would suggest at parties.

In the early fifties Herb and I lived in a small apartment on East 48th Street in Manhattan. Neither we nor our friends had much money but we all threw wine and spaghetti parties for a wonderful mix of people, all of them on the brink of being who and what they wanted to be, given time and work and luck.

"Get Shirley to read your hand. She's good at it," Herb would say.

I did a few casual readings. People with a drink in one hand and a cigarette in the other would put one or the other down and thrust a hand at me. The readings were cursory but no one seemed to care. And Herb loved the quirky quality of my abilities. I was in my early twenties and in a new and sophisticated environment. I accepted Herb's assessment. What I did was an entertainment.

Early one Sunday morning following a Saturday night party the phone rang. I answered, more than half asleep, expecting one of our mothers with bad news. Why else would anyone be calling at eight o'clock Sunday morning? Apparently my premonitions were as sleepy as I or I would have rolled over and let the phone ring.

"Shirley, this is Helen Forrest. You did my palm last night, remember?" The voice on the phone was breathy and conspiratorial.

"Yes, I remember you," I said.

I pictured her, thin and elegant in a black silk moire suit, diamond stud earrings and a remarkably beautiful gold pin in the shape of a dove on her lapel. Her hand was small and hot and in constant motion, the fingers twitching as I held it. Her feet in spike heeled black silk pumps moved against the carpet and her eyes, almost hidden behind dark bangs, flicked over my face. She was a moving target, intense, demanding, in the way she leaned toward me. I moved off, giving her a quick, glib reading. I wasn't proud of myself but I knew there would be no way to satisfy her particular hunger.

"What you told me last night was phenomenal. I *do* need more outlets for my creative energy. I *am* a warm and loving person and I *don't* have enough places to express that love. You know me. You're a wonder."

"Uh, oh," I thought as she babbled on, "I hope she didn't think I was suggesting she have an affair."

I said, "I just tell you what I see. We did talk about your possibly doing some charity work and about finding a hobby, didn't we?" I hoped we had.

She wasn't listening. She went on without a breath. "What I want to suggest is that we meet once a week, your apartment or mine, and that you continue to read me. I know my life would be enriched. I feel I could do wonderful things if you would be my palmist. Name your price, by the way. Whatever you think is fair."

This last in a whisper, so that I wondered if someone were listening, her husband or father, or someone in a white coat. I didn't have to think before I answered.

"It just doesn't work that way, Mrs. Forrest. I don't do weekly readings. Not enough changes in your life from week to week. In fact, I rarely read the same person twice. And never for money."

She didn't give up easily. We continued to talk for some minutes and in the end she hung up sounding sad rather than angry at my decision. She was the kind of needy person for whom I did not want to read ever again. One of those for whom the occult is a way to keep from coming to grips with the real world. I would avoid the Helen Forrests in future. I was learning.

On another Saturday night, in the third year of our marriage, we traveled downtown by bus from our tiny apartment to a tinier one in Greenwich Village for a party. The guests, standing elbow to elbow and hip to hip in the candlelit rooms, included actors and would-be actors, athletes, insurance salesmen, a model or two, a wife or two, only a few of whom we knew.

As soon as we came in someone called out, "Is that the girl who reads palms?" Herb answered, "Yes." Immediately I found myself in the bedroom where someone was pushing aside the coats piled on the double bed, patting the cleared space and urging me to sit. I sat. The room was darker than I would have liked, but there was a bedside table lamp which, when I clicked it on, made a pool of light on the floor and on my lap. As soon as the light went on I felt powerful. This was going to be a good night for readings.

As each person appeared out of the shadows I asked that they sit on the small straight chair that had been placed in front of me. The first few readings were good but not unusual. "How many children will I have?" "Do I have a long life line?" "'Any money in my palm?" To which I said, "Three," "Oh, yes, and a very strong health line as well," and "No, no money, but lots of ability." The people seemed pleased, but I was beginning to think this was a rather pedestrian effort on my part. I wasn't engaged. The intensity that meant I was really 'on', really connecting, was missing.

That changed when a tall, very handsome young black man stood in front of me, hesitant and quiet.

"Do you want a reading?' I asked.

"Mmm, I guess so," he said and sat in the chair. He was so tall that his knees bumped mine and he mumbled "Sorry" as he moved back.

"May I have your left hand?"

I put my own out to receive his. The hand that rested in mine was feather light despite its size, long and thin and powerful looking. Focus was instant and I was 'in' him.

"Trouble." I thought. "No wonder he was holding back."

"You have a very strong hand. Fully developed. Great health line, and look at this," I said, pointing to the two stars at the base of his middle fingers. "This means that you have two talents, two gifts that are remarkable."

I felt him responding. He didn't speak but there were waves of what felt like heat coming from him.

"You have worked hard on the one talent and virtually ignored the other. Do you have any idea what I'm talking about? Is this making any sense to you?"

"Yes," he said, "I know." He was quiet again and I took his right hand in mine.

"It's true, everything your left hand showed me. You must begin to work on this second gift or it will disappear. It's already making you unhappy," I said. That was what was clear. He was unhappy.

We were quiet. I watched him, looking down at his hands, and I felt the energy leave his body. He spoke in a whisper. "You're right. I know what you mean." Then he stood and went back to the living room. We didn't speak again.

The next few days were filled with the usual activities, producing and directing television programs at Channel 11 for Herb, and shopping, cooking, cleaning for me. Typical fifties pursuits. I would meet Herb after work and we would go for long walks through the city. We were self-absorbed and happy. The party had faded from my mind when one Friday evening the host called Herb to say that the young man for whom I had read had jumped to his death. He had been a runner, training for the Olympics, and he had wanted to be a jazz musician. His parents and his teachers and coaches, everyone whom he loved and admired had urged him to work toward the Olympics and to enjoy jazz as a hobby. He had made his own decision. His death sent me into a long period of soul searching. I felt that I had put pressure on a young man who didn't need any more pressure. What I had seen was his unhappiness. What I had not seen was his suicide. I had hoped that what I said would make it easier for him to tend to whatever it was that he loved. It hadn't and it would be nearly forty years before I would read palms again.

What changed things, made me willing to try again, was the company of a group of women writers. In my early sixties I joined a writing group which met once a week and was led by a gifted author-teacher-editor. The group, anywhere from four to seven or eight of us at a given time, was a supportive, hard working, creative and insightful gathering of women. Women came and went as changes occurred in their lives and new members joined us, but the ethos, the essence of the group remained the same. We watched each other grow and cheered each other on. We listened to one another's stories and no one laughed except in the right places. When they discovered that I had in the past read palms, they asked me to read theirs. I said no. I wasn't ready yet, even in that comfortable atmosphere.

I hadn't missed the readings in the intervening forty years. I was busy doing what I had always meant to do, raising a family. And the longer I lived, the more I experienced, the firmer became my belief in self reliance and individual responsibility. I had come far enough in my understanding to know that the young man who had taken his life all those years ago had done so on his own. Insight and experience had carried me a long way from the guilt I had felt at the time. But that didn't mean I was ready to hand out prescriptions and proscriptions to the vulnerable or to anyone who might expect a life plan from my readings. Still, in the company of women friends, I thought I might risk inviting the 'feelings' again.

One snowy evening a small event occurred which let me know I hadn't lost or forgotten the ability to go with the energy when the time was right. A writer friend had given me a ride to the house where we were meeting that night. A light snow was falling as we went in. We talked and read for two hours and then prepared to leave. My friend reached into her coat pocket for her car keys and said, "Oh, no, where are they?" She opened her purse and rummaged in it for several minutes, dumped it out on a nearby table, and went through the contents. "They're not here." Our hostess and I felt behind and under sofa cushions and looked under furniture. No keys.

"The snow is getting bad out there. Maybe we should call a cab and just get home," my friend said.

"Give me a minute to check outside," I said.

I knew where the keys were. Common sense. If they weren't where they should be, they were where they shouldn't be. But when I stepped out the front door and saw the drifts of snow, I had to admit that common sense would get me just so far. What I began to feel was the keys themselves. I walked over to a drift along the left side of the walk, bent down and reached into the snow. My fingers 'felt' the keys just before they closed around them. I went back into the house dangling the frigid keys in front of my friend. I had been so sure of finding them that I was surprised at her surprise when I was successful.

Yet when I tried several months later to locate a diamond pin for another friend, I was not successful. I could see the pin wedged between two surfaces, one hard and dirty, the other rough, like cement, but no matter how thoroughly we searched the places she had been, I could not home in on the pin. We gave up. The truth was that I had felt enormous resistance from my friend throughout the whole episode. On the one hand she seemed desperate to find the pin and on the other she did not want it back. She told me long afterward that her husband's mother had given it to her and that there had been too many emotional strings attached to the gift. She was glad it was gone.

Now that I was opening myself to possibilities again, the members of the writing group asked me to relent and read their palms. I was still reluctant. I knew them all too well to do a proper reading. But the perfect opportunity arose. Our pre-Christmas meeting was held at the new home of one of our long time members. She had built a fire in her beautiful fireplace and provided a delicious quiche and beverages in celebration of the season. We sat close to the fire and to each other, eating and talking, and when the subject of palm reading arose, I agreed. The lights were low and the firelight flickered but I could see well enough to read the hands as they were placed, one by one, in mine.

"Your hand is all potential. Almost unformed. You really must claim yourself," I said to the first, a writer of talent and insight, gentle and soft spoken, whose hand felt like the petals of a gardenia, smooth and yielding.

"I know," she said. "I do try. I will try."

There was more but what I saw in her hand was clearly a woman waiting to be born.

The next, a tall, striking, confidently successful business woman, presented a hand that was fully formed, with one glaring exception. "The drive is all there is. You are successful. You need to take time to look inward. Your hand is dry. All the energy is going out. You must save some of that energy for your own inner reservoir of strength."

"I mean to do it. Meditation, maybe. There's just so little time," she said. "But you're right. I want to pay attention to my spirit."

"You need to play," I said. "I think you've forgotten how. Meditation sounds deliberate. Not spontaneous. Try doing something outrageous on the spur of the moment."

The third reading was difficult for me. The softly blond middle-aged woman, a wife and mother, a cancer survivor, was writing an intensely personal book. It was hard for me to step back from my knowledge of her and accept what her hand would show me. The focus came and I was able to say, "You are a loving person. Not always wise in where you place your trust, but loving and forgiving. You are more than you know and who you are is growing in you. Keep remembering your strength and use it for you. That's not a selfish thing to do."

"Thank you," was all she said.

The fourth reading was the hardest. I knew this intelligent, insightful woman was resistant to what I was doing. She gave me her hand in the spirit of the evening and I thought I would not delve too deeply. I would respect her feelings.

"With what you were given in your left hand you have no business becoming what I see in your right hand. You've made this happen yourself. You've been receptive to what life has presented and have followed the leads that appeared on your way. It's an accomplished hand. It's an artistic hand, but also very practical . . . square across the base. You have three major talents, two that you know about and a third that you do not so far suspect. It will be a gift for your later life." All of this could have come from my personal experience with her, but it was also plain in her hand.

We spent the rest of the evening in relaxed enjoyment of one another's company. The aftermath of that evening was that each woman told me that I had found something true and meaningful to her. Each was making an effort to benefit from what I had seen in her hand. Good outcomes, I thought. But in August the group suffered a loss that shocked and grieved us all. The beautiful, strong young writer/business woman who was going to spend more time developing her spirit, died of a massive stroke at forty-seven. I had not seen death in her hand. I had seen only what I told her, a full life, well lived, that might benefit from some reflection. A strong reminder that whatever gift I have, it is imperfect.

Early that fall the writing group went on a long weekend to the vacation home of one of our members. We spent our time writing and reading and playing on the beach and eating in wonderful restaurants. It was a time suspended. No families, no jobs, no plans other than to enjoy the place, the time, and each other's company. One evening the possibility of a séance was raised. Would I? What would we need to have a real séance?

"I'll be happy to try," I said, surprised at the feeling of intense pleasure the request had given me. "Is there a candle in the house?"

"I'll try to find one. My father-in-law doesn't like candles around. Fire hazard," said our hostess. She went off, looking through drawers and cupboards and came back into the dining room with a fat pillar candle. "Will this do?" she asked, placing it on a saucer in the middle of the dining table.

"Perfect," I said. "Please turn off the lights and leave your watches in the living room." The thing about time, about watches and clocks, occurred to me at that moment. It was not something my grandmother had taught, but the feeling was strong. I could not have gone on with the séance had there been a marking of time near me. What my grandmother's idiosyncrasies may have been I will never know. We did not talk about them. She was my only teacher and I took what she said and did as the paradigm for psychic exploration. My own deviations from her teachings came unbidden and I accepted them as well. No watches and no clocks. We sat in the quiet room, holding hands around the table, and I began to feel the loss of control, the focused thought-without-thought, that means I'm in the right place.

"I have a feeling of peace, of forgiveness. Someone's mother," I said.

"Mine," one of the women, a gray blond, sixtyish mother and grandmother, of whom we were all fond, said. "It's my mother. I forgive her, too."

"Good," I said. "If nothing else happens tonight, that's good."

"Is my father willing to talk to me?" the woman on my right asked. She was a professor of philosophy at a local college, successful and admired by her peers. She sounded anxious and, I thought, afraid.

"I'll see," I said and let my mind search for her father. Resistance was all I felt.

"I'm sorry, he isn't willing or maybe I'm just not able to reach him," I said, not wanting to let her know I was sensing his refusal to enter in.

"I'm not surprised," she said. "Disappointed but not surprised."

"Wait, I see a piece of jewelry. A pin or a ring with a blue green stone. Lost, I think," I said. The image was not clear but the feeling around it was. Loss and sadness.

"It's my aunt's pin," the woman opposite me at the table called out. "It was lost. My grandmother gave it to her and she loved it. Can you see where it is?"

"No, I can't but it will be found. The stone is set in silver and I see it back with the one who loves it," I said.

The séance continued for another few minutes and then we all went off to bed. I slept hard and had no dreams, satisfied that I had done all I could in that other place and could now relax in the real, concrete world.

There was another incident that following winter, a feeling that came when I was unprepared. My husband and I were on a week-end vacation. I had no thoughts of readings or séances when I happened to pass through a room where the television was on. The program, a sitcom, was not one I had watched and the actor who caught my attention was no one with whom I was familiar. I remember stopping in the middle of the room, staring at the screen and in particular at a young man who was interacting with a group, hearing the laugh track and thinking, "My God, somebody help him. He's in so much trouble." The man himself, not the character he was playing. I passed it off as a momentary aberration and went on through the room to join my husband. The feeling did not fade and I looked in the TV section of the local newspaper to see what show I had been watching. Less than a week later the same show was in the news. One of the actors had committed suicide and I knew before I saw his picture which one it was. I thought of the young musician/athlete of forty years earlier and felt the same sense of helplessness and sadness. I still have no idea what to do with unbidden presentiments of trouble or danger.

One evening I had the opportunity to read the palm of a woman whom I hardly knew. She had come with several friends of mine to share a pre-holiday dinner at my home. We had enjoyed each other's company during the meal and were settled in the living room when it happened: a strong feeling that I must read this woman's hand. I hoped she would be open to the suggestion.

"Yes, of course. I'd love it," she said, holding both hands out to me as I sat next to her on the couch.

I was glad I did not know her better because the experience of reading her would be easier and clearer. No prejudgements to work around. The power of her persona reached out to me even as I took her hands and began to read. It was as if a faucet had been turned on, the flow of thoughts and words was so strong. This was one of those times when the thing does itself.

"You are totally balanced. Your hands are all but identical. You are who you were. You have great focus, ability and deliberation. And you're a nester. A home builder.

"There is a strong possibility of a deflection from your current path in life from now on. A different direction.

Soon . . . right now. It's not a depression, not a chance for the negative. It will take a great deal of energy to resist. Don't try. You will find that logic can't help you in what's to come. Use intuition, emotion.

"This change crosses everything. You can't ignore it. Stay in tune with relationships, how you feel about others and about yourself. It's a cosmic shift . . . pay attention to it. It isn't good or bad, so suspend judgment. It's something you can really sink your teeth into, something you've never thought of before with regard to yourself.

"Don't think your way through it, feel your way. It's kind of neat. Lots of stuff to go through but no disaster. Go with the flow. It will cause you to look out and what is reflected back will be a big help to you.

"You will go out of balance. We learn in disequilibrium. This state of unrest and the changes it will bring will be for your greater fulfillment. It's an opportunity. Balance, in your case, and probably in all cases implies control. Change is out of your control and therefore terrifying. If you think you know what to do, you don't. This can't be reasoned. It's way beyond that."

I thought I was finished and I let go of her hands. I felt as if I had been talking for hours but it had been only about ten minutes. I began to talk again. There was more that she should hear.

"I'm still tuning in. It's still really active. It's as if you had suddenly said 'All those things that I thought were not a part of me, were not important to me . . . *are* a part of me.' They are. Understand and embrace them. All of your conscious life, that stuff you have so well under control, is the light side of the moon, known and familiar. At the edge, where it starts to get dark, lie dragons, the edge of the map, the place beyond where you have walked. But that place exists. Its' huge and it won't be denied. You haven't begun to know the territory that is you. You need to get closer to a dream state. Don't push any thoughts away. Go without a plan. Everything is permitted, encouraged, to be explored. There is no mother around . . . you can do what you want. When you find it, it will feed you. It will be a jewel and you will want to claim it."

It is rare that I remember the details of what passes between me and the person being read, but one of the women present, a close friend of the woman whom I read, wrote down most of what I said. Because, she said, I had been so completely on the mark, she made her notes available to me and I decided to include them here.

None of this is remarkable. Paying attention to and drawing inferences from the world around us is something we all do every day, every moment. It is how we exist in the real world. Some of us do it better than others but I think we could all improve our skills in this regard.

Other people do amazing things: reaching the dead, predicting down to the nano second what one's life will be, charting the influence of the stars. I have no quarrel with them. Still, my own doubts persist. I pose questions and I have no answers. I am unsure of a life after death, so with whom am I connecting in a séance? I trust only those things which I can put to the test of logic and yet I believe in fairies. I've seen them, graceful, transparent, shy. I fear and distrust cults of the mind and spirit, yet I read the palms of my friends, people whom I love and respect, and I give them advice and counsel. I don't read the palms of my family. And I don't read for money. The limits are my own. I continue to respond to my spirit and I continue to be ambivalent about sharing the messages I receive. One thing I'm sure of. My long dead psychic grandmother is proud of me. She told me so. Really.

HALF MOON SOUP

Anima Mundi: Soul of the World. Her pubis and left breast are represented as half moons.

in a hot skillet
brown cubed chuck
and chopped onion

overcast bonechill damp
soup day
scent of meat and onion inspires the cook
and spurs her on
with promises beyond the pot

deglaze the pan with dry sherry

crisp meaty bits
carameled in onion sugar
spit and sizzle when the sherry hits
bubble blend send up a vapor
intimate insistent
the cook inhales
incense, she thinks

place all in large kettle with beef or chicken stock

this cauldron
serious heavy too big for everyday
has held three pounds of pasta at one time
chili enough for New Year's Eve,
the cook remembers
no task too onerous
now it opens wide for half moon soup
and settles down to business

add sliced vegetables cut thick enough to keep their shape

the cook's heart quickens
from here on what is next
is anybody's guess
pot luck, she says, rummaging the vegetable bin
she finds parsnips and mushrooms
celery and faintly purple turnip globes
she splits and slices them in half moons
their lunar faces palest white and celadon
she adds them to the pot by spilling handsful
catch as catch can
trusting synergy

add barley

the cook sifts labial barley buds
through careful fingers
into plop plop liquid lava
primal soup, she says

season with pepper garlic
dill or summer savory
what you will
to taste

no formula for seasoning save alchemy
at table each who tastes will murmur
sage
oregano
one will state emphatically
with the gourmand's certainty
chervil and thyme
the cook will keep her counsel

bring to a boil
simmer for one hour

the cook knows
   waiting whets the appetite for more than soup

add crushed tomatoes
simmer one quarter of an hour
serve with a hearty bread

the cook will fill your bowl
   step back
   and wait for you to breathe the rising fragrance
   fill the harvest spoon and lift it to your mouth
   swallow down and smack your lips
   break bread for sopping up

   now thank the cook for half moon soup

   she will take your empty bowl as votive offering
   then resting on her three-leg kitchen stool
   arms folded on her breast
   she will say
   soup is a blessing on a bone chill day

THE TUSCAN SUN

good morning, I say to the old man who was born in Italy
buon giorno, Signorina. I know you ?
across his waist high suburban wire fence
we greet each other
he preens his barber trimmed mustache
and squints a smile at me
an ancient satyr with a good memory
no, signor, but I know you.
my smile flirtatious out of courtesy
and in honor of the laughing boy
who flirts with me from his black eyes
I know you from the statue of Our Lady
in the corner there, beside the azalea
and from the grape vine growing over your back door
from the flowers everywhere
I know you because I have seen you in Tuscany
a hundred times
in piazzas and cafes sipping espresso
watching the dark eyed girls
your portrait hangs in the Ufizzi
I know you
your cheeks are tan with remembered sun
surely no summer here in this unfriendly latitude
has burned you brown
I know you
the plaster fawn grazing on your perfect grass
reminds me of Michaelangelo

as he is meant to do
not art, but the suggestion
in case too many years make you forget
the place of sun and wine and statuary
where you were young and strong and irresistible
I know you
he has not moved
has listened hard, translating as he goes
to think how it would sound in Italian
all that I have said

gracie, Signorina
when you pass this way again, come in
we have a glass of wine

the next time I am in the neighborhood
I see that the house is in new hands
Our Lady and the fawn are gone
the flowers riot on their own
and the grapevine languishes
he is not here
he is in Italy, I tell myself
and turn away
remembering the taste of vino
and the touch of the Tuscan sun

BASIL'S WORLD

Basil's world has shrunk to a wheel chair
and three plastic bags tied to the arms
    against certain theft
he carries three Bic lighters and a pack of Marlboroughs
a box of Kleenex
two boxes of cough drops one Hall's one Luden's
at the bottom of one bag is a set of keys
they belong to the Lincoln he was driving
when he had the stroke
his sister sold the car and kept the money
    for him, she said
he has two Western novels in one bag
I read them to him when I visit
mostly we talk
but only of the time before
when he was whole
he was a sailor and there is the smell of brine about him
his beard
which I trim every now and then to keep it trig
is grey and strong
stronger than he but not greyer
it is a beard to wear on deck and in the wind

Basil is brusque and arch
and flirtatious with me
showing me the man under the dying flesh
eyes fierce with life and lust
and anger
we sit in the day room, marina of moored wheel chairs
we lock eyes when we talk to shut out all but the past
I have come to need his vital life
his strong and absolute denial
so I can come to this place of final days
with cheer and hope
to share the world outside with those who must know
      that it incredibly exists without them

on Tuesday when I come as usual
I ask at the desk for Basil
he died in his sleep on Sunday night, the woman says
I am not his next of kin except in all that matters
I was not called
too late anyway
I am saddened for myself
pushing back death alone is tiring work
and lonely

but the sailor sleeps
and I am the last girl in the last port

HAROLD GODFREY MONTGUMERY

Memoir

Harold Godfrey Montgumery (the spelling is his) was fifty-four years old and averse to taking baths. He kept his crumpled hat on in the house against my mother's wishes and he never groomed his graying, scraggly moustache. Most of the time I loved him dearly, but there were long stretches of days and weeks when I was angry with him. Never enough to provoke a fight. He might leave, after all, and find another eight-year-old girl to live with. My anger stemmed from a certain air of indifference on Montgumery's part. He was never called Harold Godfrey. Always just Montgumery. Sometimes I suspected him of liking my mother better than he liked me.

"Does Montgumery want any supper, Shirley?" she would say. She always had an extra chair at the table just in case.

I would lift the corner of the table cloth, look closely for my friend in the dim light, and, if he was there I would interpret for him.

"Yes, he says he's hungry."

"Well, then, he'll have to go wash his hands and take off his hat and sit up at the table like everybody else."

"Okay, Mommy. He's back and his hands are clean and he has his hat off and he wants soup," I would say, hoping that it was true that I was the only one who could see him, because he certainly had not washed his hands nor taken off his hat, though he certainly did want soup.

I would have said at the time that he was a good friend of mine, but the truth is he was casual about our relationship, not to say cavalier. Showing up when it pleased him and not necessarily when I wanted a playmate. Leaving in the middle of things without explanation. Still, he was undemanding and quietly companionable when it suited him. He stayed around through most of my ninth year, though when the going got rough and my parents separated for six weeks, he made himself scarce. Montgumery could not handle seeing me sad. He left for good in typical fashion just before I turned ten, no forewarning and no word of him since.

MY MOTHER'S BODY

Memoir

"The nurses think I have beautiful feet. The feet of a much younger woman," said my mother in her ninetieth year, in her room in the nursing home, in the full pride of her surprising vanity.

Three years later she would enter a morphine world of old friends and family members long dead and encounters with Death with whom she argued and whom she took to task for his heartlessness and for his sloppy system of pick up and delivery.

"He just stood there in the doorway and did nothing. I called to him but he wouldn't come in and he wouldn't go away. What kind of a way is that to run a business?"

When he did finally come into the room she was silent and more than ready to accompany him. She was cremated according to her own plans. "How Great Thou Art" and "Send in the Clowns" were played at the church service, and we all, her family and friends, went in to the church hall for the funeral collation. Again, everything according to her plans and wishes. We drove in our several cars to the burial ground, the occupants of the car in which I rode recalling Mother's humor, her quirks, her kindness. We laughed and didn't cry until the small gold colored urn she had purchased for her ashes years ago was deposited in the ground beside my father's grave.

Now we were free to go home and grieve in whatever way would serve us, in whatever way we could. Or not, if we had already come to terms with her absence or if, as was unlikely, she had meant little enough so that she could be consigned to the back closet of memory to be pulled forward at family gatherings or at church services where the dead may be remembered.

Over the weeks and months I found that I had easy access to her words, to our life experience, to her essence. I could consult her, laugh with her, listen to her as easily as when she was alive. More easily now that the mother/daughter thing was solved, dissolved, melted and resolved. Our having been together in the world until I was seventy two had given us the time we needed to work through the slights, the misunderstandings, the jealousies and mistrust that had cropped up on both sides over the years. We parted friends, loving and appreciating one another.

What struck me with a force that had the surprise of ambush was the absence of her body, the emptiness of the space she had occupied. It is not too much to say that my eyes began to ache for the sight of her. How could she not be sitting propped on three pillows, reading in bed, in the bed I inherited from her and in which I sleep every night? How could she not be bending over the second drawer of the sideboard putting away her silver, the silver I use for every family dinner? How can I hang clothes on the line to flap and dry in the breeze off the Atlantic and she not be there to hold the other end of the sheet, to take the wooden clothes pin from between her teeth and snap it on the double fold of bleached white cotton to hold it against that breeze?

I remember the womb, the soft, strong rhythms, the warmth and the sudden, hard expulsion. We were one and then we were two, our bodies separate and the air between ringing with her screams. I remember the feel of her bare skin, her breast given for my nourishment. Common wisdom says that I can't remember that far back, but my knowledge is deeper, truer. It is in my body.

As I grew I was never far from the feel and the sight of her physical presence. Her hands were soft, gentle, bathing me, combing my hair. Kind. Her slender, expressive hands, scrubbed and ironed and changed the linens and chopped the wood and tended the coal stove and the boiler and never lost their gentleness. I did not learn my abrupt, impatient moves from her.

Her skin tanned in an instant so that people speculated as to whether she might be part Indian. Yet to the very end it was silken as if it had been talcum powdered the moment before you touched her hand, her cheek. She was solid, present, without being fat, thin only in times of crisis. When my father left her for another woman she became a wraith. He came back and she bloomed. When her second husband was dying and she had told him she no longer loved him but that she would see him through to death, she was a wisp. Two months after he was safely gone she bloomed again. Her body a signal to the world: I'm fine. I'm in pain. I'm fine again.

Her hair, abundant, shining, invited me as a small girl to run a comb through it, to tangle my fingers in it. Sepia pictures of her as a flapper show her hair close cut in what was called a boyish bob. Flappers cut their hair, bound their breasts and tried to look like adolescents but the photos show my mother as a woman, rounded and feminine. When I was six or seven and we camped beside a lake or river for the summer she would let her then long hair loose, to her waist. Auburn, my father called the color. Dark brown with mahogany lights. For me, her hair free of pins was what the freedom of summer felt like. And when she was old and her hair was white it still jumped with energy under the brush and framed her face with softness.

She and I shared a bed after my father's early death. I hated it at first, the sagging of the mattress in her direction, the sounds and smells of another person in my space, but I soon came to wait for her to come to bed. The sheets were cold in our unheated third floor bedroom and she radiated warmth. When I had a bad dream I had only to reach a few inches to put my arm around her waist and fall asleep again without disturbing her. I was safe with my body close to hers. No room for fear in the same bed.

Now I want that space that was hers to be filled with her solid, corporeal presence. I've lost others dearly loved and have missed them, wanted them back, but nothing hinted at the void the dissolution of the body of my genesis would leave. I began there, in that flesh, but I can't end there. I'm on my own and my body is sending messages I'm not ready to receive.

THE COWBOY

A Daughter Remembers Her Father

One leg was flesh and blood and cartilage and one was wood and leather and metal. My father unstrapped the man-made leg at night and stood it in the corner of the bedroom he shared with my mother. Shared most of the time, when he wasn't flying off somewhere on business, monkey and otherwise. Wood and leather and metal did not seem to deter the 'dirty blond in Dayton' or any of the other women who found my father as tempting as a banana split or a double old fashioned made with hooch aged in the bathtub for a week. Delectable. Irresistible. My mother found him all of that and more. Frustrating, infuriating, flash-tempered and beautiful beyond her country dreams. He yo-yoed her on a string of charm. She left and came back, left and came back. Where else on God's earth would she find this incandescence, this fire of a man.

His brain worked beyond the speed of light. Nearly everyone he knew was, in comparison, slow, especially his children and his wife.

"Dont'cha get it?"

I didn't get it or not all of it. Not enough to share his excitement. Not enough to ask the right questions. How carefully and with what pleasure he led us through Einstein's Theory of Relativity. All I remember is something about a fly riding on a train. With his pale white, square tipped fingers he would trace his own beautiful schematics for one of his many inventions, taking us through his thought processes as he developed the idea, showing us how this cam and that drive shaft would work when he had enough money to build the prototype. We brushed our teeth with an electric tooth brush of his design and craftsmanship in nineteen-thirty-seven when I was ten. He showed us drawings for an air-cooled aircraft engine in the early thirties, long before we could have understood anything but the rare and precious time we were sharing with him. I ached to follow where he led, to gain his approbation, his white-toothed, full of glee smile that came so easily when he was pleased. It didn't happen often. Just often enough to keep me trying.

People often used the word genius to describe our father. It didn't seem right then and it doesn't now. I think of those who are true geniuses as focused on the field of their particular gift. Dad's field was the universe. Anything that came to hand was worth figuring out, tinkering with, improving on. And if it hadn't been thought of by someone else, so much the better. Making a life size paper mache horse's head to wear for Halloween was as engrossing to him as building a house trailer or a log cabin, or designing and building a low wing monoplane.

His sense of humor, too, kept us from thinking of him as a genius. In the winter of nineteen-thirty-seven Dad went down to his basement workshop and built a pair of wooden feet. He nailed ovals of wood to the bottom surface of the foot sized wooden forms to suggest the pads of a lion or tiger paw. He nailed wide rawhide straps to each side of the form for attaching them to one's overshoes. One moonlit night, after a deep snowfall, he drove to a field, put on his lion feet and walked the length of the field and into the woods beyond. He took off the feet and circled around to his car, careful not to leave human tracks anywhere except the road. Then he called the police and the newspaper and told them he had seen a strange cat-like creature roaming the field in the moonlight, too large an animal to be anything but an escaped lion or some such beast. In the ensuing days, a herd of hunters showed up at our doorstep and Dad led them out to the field where the animal's footprints were frozen into the snow. I remember how seriously he told them to be very quiet and very, very cautious. This was a big one, this Glawackus. The name was his, a contraction of the town we lived in, Glastonbury, and wacky. The papers printed the story and I don't remember his ever retracting it or explaining what he had done to anyone except his closest friends. My brother and I each have one of the lion's paws and I laugh every time I look at it. No one I've ever known has taken such elaborate pains to play a trick on the world except my father. I'm as proud of him for that as for any other thing.

The shiny sepia photos of him that lie in a shoe box waiting to be seen to are cracked and curled. We have other pictures of our father and mother, my brother and I, that are framed and properly cared for, but the ones I'm thinking of show Dad in full cowboy regalia. In one he's standing on the platform beside a train with a large group of people. They are laughing and they have their arms around each other's shoulders. The women are in long coats with fur collars. It is the late twenties or the very early thirties and Dad appears to be the host. He is the only one in costume. He doesn't think of it as costume, the plaid shirt, the bandana around the neck, the full chaps, and the Stetson. The only things missing are the cowboy boots. His artificial leg would make high heeled boots impossible to walk in. There are other pictures over the course of his short life that show him in partial cowboy gear, the shirt, the wide leather belt, and always the Stetson. He was outrageously handsome in the Stetson and his grin tells you that he knew it.

He read Zane Gray and Bret Harte and adventure magazines like Blue Book and Argosy. On the nights when he was home to put us to bed he read us tales of King Arthur and the Round Table or he told of Pecos Bill or Paul Bunyan, not the usual stories but ones he made up as he went along, his voice tense with excitement in the darkened bedroom I shared with my brother. The details in his stories, the sound of the wolves and coyotes, the beaded loin cloths of the Indians, the sun glinting on the coats of mail worn in the lists, were so convincing that I believed he had, in some other life, lived each of the adventures he told us. When our mother read to us it was Pooh and A Child's Garden of Verses. Our father sent us off to sleep with guns and lances and horses racing over deserts and heroes in white hats or golden crowns 'nick-of-timing' it to the rescue. We did not have night mares.

Adventure was all. Dad knew from very early on that his life would in all likelihood be short. He had severe and debilitating asthma which began when he was in his late teens and which prevented him from finishing college. Oxygen tents, needles, bottles of adrenalin, were always near at hand. Ambulances took him away in the night time after time and brought him home again to be nursed back to reasonable health by our mother. Death was often as close as the next attempt to breathe. He did not complain. I don't mean he didn't say he was tired or that he never said "This damned asthma". What I mean is, he didn't blame God or Fate or whatever it was that took his leg and his breath. He knew that life is the only adventure and while he could, he would have at it. The frontier that he took to was the sky. He became a pilot. The world of seat-of-the-pants flying and derring-do and barn-storming suited him. He loved the near brushes with danger, the sudden fogs, the forced landings in pastures, the comraderie of his fellow flyers. And he dearly loved his jodhpurs, his leather helmet and goggles, his leather jacket. Flying was a great life for a show-off with a brilliant, inventive, hungry mind and spirit. If he was disappointed not to have lived through the settling of the Wild West, I know he counted himself lucky to have been born into the age of flight. Still, he'd have made a hell of a cowboy.

ACKNOWLEDGEMENTS

With gratitude to all who have taught me life lessons: every member of my family, those here now and those who came before; all of my friends, some of whom you will meet in the pages of this book; Linsey Abrams, Edith Chevat, Betsy Harding, Ann Breen Metcalf and Barbara Roberts, those writers of talent, insight and compassion, who join all of the above mentioned in being a part of this book and of my life. Each of them has helped me find some piece of myself, even those bits I didn't know were lost. Thank you, all.